G000270881

DAN TOOMBS

THE CURRY GUY VEGGIE

Over 100 vegetarian Indian restaurant classics and new dishes to make at home

Photography by Kris Kirkham

Hardie Grant
QUADRILLE

For Caroline, Katy, Joe
and Jennifer

CONTENTS

PREFACE

Cooking has been a passion of mine for as long as I can remember. I love the thrill of mixing spices and other ingredients to create delicious, homemade feasts for family and friends. For the past 25 years, my main food obsession has been Indian food. There is always something new to learn and another exciting mouthful to enjoy.

It wasn't just the amazing flavours and textures that fuelled my desire to learn more. It was the way you could cook from a list of exotic ingredients to create a popular dish and then tweak the recipe ever so slightly to come up with another that was equally colourful and tasty.

If, like me, you've taken your search for the perfect Indian meal beyond what is on offer at the traditional British curry house, you aren't alone! I recently took a couple trips out to India with the sole purpose of comparing what I had learned and made at home with what was being served out there. Luckily, the most popular and authentic Indian dishes have now made their way to the UK and beyond, and it is my goal with this cookbook to demonstrate just how quickly and easily you can master them at home.

You might know that my first cookbook, *The Curry Guy*, was mostly about the recipes many of us have grown to love at our favourite local curry houses. My second, *The Curry Guy Easy*, continued on that topic but a few more recipes from the new and hugely popular Indian-run restaurants made their way onto the pages – all simplified for the home cook. Now, I've gone all out to give you the recipes for the 'must try' vegetarian dishes being served all round the country. These dishes are in such high demand that even the most traditional British curry houses are finding it essential to up their game with their vegetarian dishes. Imagine being able to whip up these mouth-watering Indian meals whenever you want. This collection of recipes should give you what you're looking for.

When I first mentioned on social media that I wanted to write a vegetarian Indian cookbook, the response was fantastic! There were a few hardened carnivores out there, however, who gave it to me plain and simple: there was no way they would be purchasing *that* book! I took that as a challenge. Some of the best vegetarian food in the world comes from India and I didn't want them to miss out. Hopefully, they and you will trust me on this one and give these recipes a go.

Many of my dishes are also vegan, and where they're not I've given 'make it vegan' variations if possible so you can still enjoy most recipes if you're egg- and dairy-free.

Personally, I have loved every minute of writing and developing the recipes here. Believe me, it took some time to get them just right but there was never a dull moment. I found it fascinating that many of these recipes had been around in some shape or form for hundreds of years but so many of them were new to me. I hope you find the process of preparing different ingredients in lots of different ways as enlightening as I did.

One thing I would like to stress is that some of the best recipes take time to prepare. The actual work involved, however, is not difficult. I have attempted to keep the recipes as authentic as possible, though at times I couldn't help but throw in a few curve balls. I'm not going to mention them here but hope you enjoy them if you encounter one or two.

I'm @TheCurryGuy on Twitter, Facebook and Instagram, and I'm happy to answer recipe questions. You might also like to watch my new YouTube channel, where I demonstrate the recipes in my books. Here's the link: www.youtube.com/c/dantoombs

Happy Cooking!

Dan

GETTING THE MOST FROM THIS BOOK

Many people find the idea of cooking Indian food a bit daunting. They falsely believe that there are too many ingredients and techniques for the meal to ever go right! However, the required cooking techniques are mostly quite simple. A few things, like making dosas, might take a little practice to get right, but even if your thin and crispy dosas look more like fat pancakes, you'll still end up with a delicious meal. Also, although many of the ingredients in the following recipes might be new to you, you'll find that most of them are used in different ways and are therefore good to have at hand. For this reason, I have included on pages 152–55 a list of ingredients you will want to purchase in large or small quantities, depending on how often you want to enjoy amazing home-cooked Indian food.

To get the most out of this cookbook, there are a few things you can do to make the following recipes even better and easier.

1) **Fresh is usually best:** One of the most important things you can do for optimum flavour, texture and visual appeal is use the freshest ingredients. You might be happy to hear, however, that you can often save time and cheat while getting even better results. Using frozen spinach or tinned (canned) tomatoes, for example, can add amazing colour to a dish with no loss of flavour or goodness. I prefer dried beans that I soak and cook myself, but tinned (canned) are a good substitute. I wrote all the recipes as I make them at home, using the ingredients fresh, frozen or tinned as I feel work best, but feel free to adjust these recipes to better suit how you cook or what you have on hand.

2) **Get your ingredients ready before you start:** At my cookery classes, many people are surprised at how simple it is to whip up an amazing curry even when the recipe calls for a lot of 'exotic' ingredients. The key to ease and success is getting everything prepared before you start cooking. You don't want to be burning your delicious tempered spices while you're looking for an onion to chop in the next step. Simply prepare the ingredients and place them in the order you will be using them. You then only need to read the recipe and add the ingredients when required.

3) **Get the recipe right for you:** I recommend tasting the food as you cook it. This will help you memorize the flavours of the different spices and other ingredients you add and make it possible for you to adjust the recipes to taste. These are all authentic recipes but cooking them to your liking will not make them any less authentic. Don't be a slave to the recipes. If you feel more chilli powder will make the dish better, add it. If you prefer fresh chopped tomatoes to tinned (canned), go for it. My recipes evolve over time and I change them often. You can do the same so that they are perfect for you.

RECIPE LABELS

I have labelled each recipe with one or more symbols to better help you find the ones you want to try.

30 mins or less: Look for this when you want to whip something up quickly.

Low and slow: A longer cooking time is essential for these recipes but the work involved is usually quite simple.

Fermenting or soaking time required: Fermenting different batters and pastes is key to getting 'that flavour'.

Vegan: There are many vegan recipes in the book – look for this symbol. There are also many recipes that can easily be made vegan – look for the 'Make it vegan' instructions at the bottom of the recipe.

Gluten-free: I am always asked which of my recipes are gluten-free. Most are. Look for this symbol.

STORING FOOD AND WORKING AHEAD

STORING SPICES

Whole spices stay fresh for a very long time. Once opened, it is best to store them in a cool, dark location in air-tight containers. When they are ground, spices lose their pungency much faster, but homemade spices will last longer than anything you purchase off the shelf. Try making one or all of the spice blends overleaf – they have a real kick to them once ground. That powerful aroma only lasts for about a day but the flavour should last for at least three months if stored correctly.

STORING SAUCES

Sometimes it's convenient to work ahead. The curry sauces in this book can be made up to three days before serving and stored in the fridge. Most also freeze well, although I don't recommend freezing those containing dairy.

STORING RICE, PULSES AND LENTILS

Don't go by the 'best before' date on these! Rice actually gets better with age. Store rice and pulses in an air-tight container in a dark location. Beans and lentils in particular play a big part in many of my recipes, and you will save a lot of money by purchasing them dry, soaking them and cooking as per the packet or recipe instructions. I usually cook the whole bag and use leftovers for other recipes or freeze them. Both cooked beans and lentils freeze well. Generally speaking, dried lentils and beans double in weight and size when cooked. So a recipe requiring 200g (1 cup) of cooked lentils will need 100g (½ cup) dried.

STORING HERBS

Green herbs like coriander, mint and methi freeze really well. If I have some that aren't so fresh, I blend them with a little water then freeze them in ice cube trays. These small herb cubes are great added to curry sauces – they are almost as good as fresh herbs.

STORING PICKLES

To keep your pickles fresh, store them in sterilized jars... Rinse the jars in hot, soapy water, then rinse and drain. Preheat your oven to 130°C (250°F/Gas 1). Place the jars in the oven and let them heat for about 15 minutes. Carefully remove them from the oven and fill them while still hot.

PREPARATION RECIPES

The following spice blends and products are used a lot in this collection of recipes. Buy them or make them – you decide. For me...? There's nothing quite as good as homemade.

GARAM MASALA SPICE BLEND

MAKES 170G (1½ CUPS)

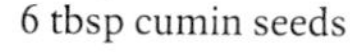

6 tbsp coriander seeds
6 tbsp cumin seeds
5 tsp black peppercorns
4 tbsp fennel seeds
3 tsp cloves
7.5cm (3in) piece of cinnamon stick
5 dried bay leaves
20 green cardamom pods
2 large pieces of mace

Toast all the spices in a dry frying pan over medium–high heat until fragrant and warm to touch but not yet smoking, moving them around in the pan and being careful not to burn them. If they begin to smoke, take them off the heat. Tip the warm spices onto a plate and leave to cool.

When cool, grind the spices to a fine powder in a spice grinder or with a pestle and mortar.

Store in an air-tight container in a cool, dark place and use within 2 months for optimal flavour.

CHAAT MASALA SPICE BLEND

MAKES 160G (SCANT 1¼ CUPS)

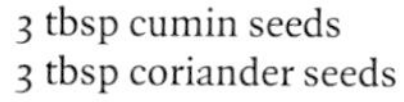

3 tbsp cumin seeds
3 tbsp coriander seeds
1 tsp chilli powder
4 tbsp amchoor (dried mango powder)
3 tbsp powdered black salt
1 tbsp freshly ground black pepper
A pinch of asafoetida (please be aware that some brands may contain gluten)
1 tbsp dried mint (optional)
1 tbsp garlic powder
1 tsp ajwain (carom) seeds

Toast the cumin and coriander seeds in a dry frying pan over medium heat until fragrant and warm to the touch but not yet smoking, moving them around in the pan and being careful not to burn them. Tip the spices onto a plate and leave to cool slightly.

When cool, grind the roasted seeds to a fine powder in a spice grinder or with a pestle and mortar. Add the remaining ingredients and grind some more until you have a very fine powder.

Store in an air-tight container in a cool, dark place and use within 2 months for optimal flavour.

TANDOORI MASALA POWDER

MAKES 120G (SCANT 1 CUP)

This is in a few recipes in this book and can be added (to taste) to other dishes for more zing!

3 tbsp coriander seeds
3 tbsp cumin seeds
1 tbsp black mustard seeds
5cm (2in) piece of cinnamon stick
3 dried bay leaves
Small piece of mace
2 tbsp finely ground garlic powder
2 tbsp dried onion powder
1 tbsp ground ginger
2 tbsp amchoor (dried mango powder)

Roast the whole spices in a dry frying pan over medium-high heat until warm to the touch and fragrant, but not yet smoking. Be careful not to burn the spices. Tip onto a plate to cool.

Grind to a fine powder in a spice grinder or pestle and mortar and tip into a bowl. Stir in the garlic and onion powders, ginger and amchoor.

Store in an air-tight container in a cool, dark place. Use within 2 months for optimal flavour.

GARLIC AND GINGER PASTE

Simply blend equal amounts of garlic and ginger with a little water until you have a paste. Done!

Keep, covered in the fridge, for up to 3 days or freeze in small batches. The paste may turn a little blue or green after a day or two in the fridge but this doesn't affect the flavour and is perfectly safe. It is less likely to turn green if you use older garlic.

YOUR THREE HOUSE SAUCES

Here's something you may or may not have noticed. Every good authentic Indian restaurant has a selection of house sauces that they serve in many different ways. More often than not, the following three sauces – mint and coriander sauce, tamarind sauce and yoghurt sauce – are part of (or the whole) selection. This isn't only here in the UK but in India too.

These three sauces are served as dips with papadams, dosas, idlis and samosas, and are a must drizzled over chaats, sandwiches and wraps. So think of these sauces as your own 'house sauces', as you'll be using them a lot in this book.

You can find each of these in bottles at Asian shops, but they are so easy to make. The tamarind sauce will keep in the fridge indefinitely, so I always have some of that on hand.

MINT AND CORIANDER SAUCE

MAKES 250ML (1 CUP)

This is a sauce I make all the time. It is so versatile, I decided I'd better just start my book off with this most delicious and easy of sauces! For convenience, I store it in a squeeze bottle, but that isn't essential.

Mint and coriander (cilantro) sauce is available at Asian shops but nothing beats taking it all up a notch with your own homemade version. You can adjust the recipe too, as you will see in some of the later recipes. Vary the coriander-to-mint ratio, add more or less chillies, use yoghurt or leave it out... this sauce is a good'n!

2 tsp cumin seeds
1 very large bunch fresh mint, about 100g (3½oz)
1 very large bunch fresh coriander (cilantro), about 100g (3½oz)
6 green chillies (more or less to taste)
4 garlic cloves
5cm (2in) piece of ginger
Juice of 2 lemons
150g (scant ⅓ cup) plain yoghurt (shop-bought or make your own – see below, optional)
Salt

In a dry frying pan, roast the cumin seeds over medium–high heat until warm to the touch and fragrant but not yet smoking.

Pour the roasted seeds into a blender or spice grinder with the mint, coriander (cilantro), green chillies, garlic, ginger, lemon juice and 2 tablespoons of the yoghurt, if using. Blend to a paste. If you are having trouble getting the ingredients to blend, add a little more lemon juice or a drop or two of water until you have a thick green paste.

You could now use the sauce to spread over sandwiches and wraps but if you are making chaats or like a smoother, thinner sauce, whisk the remaining yoghurt into the paste until very smooth. (You could even add more yoghurt if you prefer.) Season with salt to taste.

I like to store this sauce for up to 3 days in restaurant-style squirt bottles for squeezing over lots of different dishes.

MAKE IT VEGAN

You could either leave out the yoghurt for a stronger but very delicious flavour or try a soy or coconut yoghurt.

YOGHURT SAUCE

MAKES 500ML (2 CUPS)

500g (2 cups) plain natural yoghurt
Juice of 1 lime
½–1 tsp chilli powder (or to taste)
Chaat masala and/or salt to taste

Place all the ingredients in a mixing bowl and whisk until creamy smooth. Taste and add more salt or spices to your liking.

Keep it in the fridge until required.

MAKE IT VEGAN

Soy or coconut yoghurt can be used instead of dairy yoghurt.

TAMARIND SAUCE

MAKES 250ML (1 CUP)

There are many brands of tamarind sauce that you can purchase to make life easy. They are good but most are a lot sweeter than this version. I don't really have a sweet tooth and prefer the very tart flavour of this tamarind sauce. You could, of course, add more sugar or jaggery to taste. One thing is certain: when you make your own tamarind sauce, your dishes will taste better!

This is a sauce I always have on hand and I store it in a convenient squirt bottle. It keeps forever in the fridge and is delicious added to chaats, wraps and curries.

200g (7oz) block of tamarind pulp
1 tsp ground cumin
1 tsp chaat masala (optional)
½ tsp ground ginger
½ tsp chilli powder (or to taste)
1 tbsp sugar or jaggery (more or less to taste)
Salt

Break the block of tamarind into about 6 pieces, put in a small saucepan and cover with 375ml (1½ cups) water. Bring to a rolling simmer over medium–high heat, stirring often, for about 5 minutes, then remove from the heat and let it cool for another 5 minutes.

Using a wooden spoon or potato masher, smash the tamarind in the water. The sauce will become thick, like ketchup. Run this through a sieve into a bowl, pushing against the solids with a spoon as you do. You should end up with a thick paste. If you have ever used shop-bought tamarind concentrate, this is what you have – though shop-bought concentrate is much more concentrated. Discard any solids that remain in the sieve.

Return the tamarind paste to the saucepan and add the cumin, chaat masala (if using), ginger, chilli powder and sugar. Bring to a simmer for about 3 minutes, until the sugar is completely dissolved. You can add a drop more water if you prefer a runnier sauce or reduce it more if you prefer a thicker sauce. Taste the sauce and add more sugar, salt or other spices to taste. (You will need to dissolve any additional sugar over medium heat if added.)

SNACKS AND STARTERS

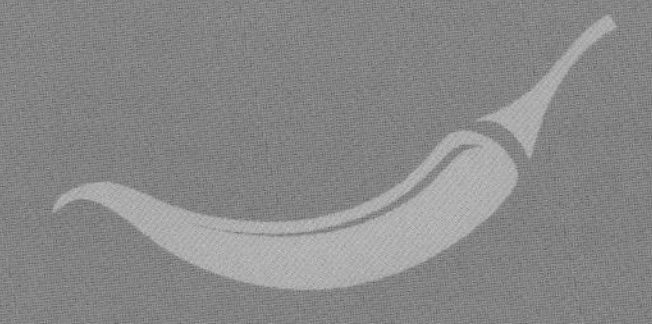

A selection of snacks is the perfect way to start an Indian meal. I've collected and further developed these recipes over the years and hope you'll enjoy them as much as I do. I make them all the time. They provide perfect nibbles for nights in front of the TV or even packed up and assembled for a day outing. Perhaps the samosas are best eaten hot, but I've had a few cold and wasn't disappointed!

POSH BOMBAY MIX

SERVES 4 AS A SNACK

Delicious served with drinks before a meal, you simply have to try this posh Bombay mix (shown on page 15). This one really packs a punch! Use the Bombay mix of your choice. You'll find the best selection at Asian grocers but it is also available in supermarkets. If eating gluten-free is important, be sure to check the bag, as some can contain gluten.

PREP TIME: 10 MINS

A few large handfuls of your Bombay mix of choice
1–2 green chillies, finely chopped
3 tbsp finely chopped coriander (cilantro) stems
1/4 red onion, finely chopped
1/2 tomato, deseeded and diced
1/2 tbsp mustard oil
1/2 tsp chaat masala
1 tbsp lemon juice

Using a cocktail mixer or any container with a firm-fitting lid, add your favourite Bombay mix along with the rest of the ingredients. Close the lid and shake hard.

Eat immediately or the Bombay mix will get soggy.

TAJAH BADAM

(SPICY BANGLADESHI ALMONDS)

SERVES 4–6 AS A SNACK

I love bringing this tasty snack out when we have friends over. It's always devoured and only takes a few minutes to throw together. It is pictured on page 15.

PREP TIME: 5 MINS
COOKING TIME: 2 MINS

1 tbsp rapeseed (canola) oil
250g (3 cups) flaked (slivered) almonds
4 long green chillies, finely sliced lengthwise
A pinch of ground turmeric
Juice of 1 lime
Salt
3 tbsp chopped coriander (cilantro), to serve

Heat the oil in a large frying pan. Add the almonds and toast for about 1 minute, until lightly browned. Add the chillies and turmeric and stir to combine.

Serve on a warmed plate with the lime juice squeezed over the top and salt to taste. Garnish with the chopped coriander (cilantro).

MASALA PAPADS

SERVES 2 OR MORE AS PART OF A MULTI-COURSE MEAL

I think you'll like these roasted papads topped with this simple but tasty masala. I like to stack them up and serve them like a salad, but simply topping a papad with the masala is equally as good. They are pictured on page 15. You can prepare them a couple of days ahead: just store the roasted papads in an air-tight container and the masala in the fridge.

PREP TIME: 10 MINS
COOKING TIME: 10 MINS

1 large tomato, diced
½ red onion, finely chopped
2–3 green chillies, finely chopped
Juice of 1 lime
3 tbsp finely chopped coriander (cilantro)
Salt and freshly ground black pepper
½ tsp chaat masala (optional)
3–4 tbsp rapeseed (canola) oil
2–3 papads per person

Mix the tomato, red onion, chillies, lime juice and coriander (cilantro) in a large bowl. Season with salt and pepper to taste and add a little chaat masala if you like. Remember that most papads and chaat masala (if using) already have salt in them, so it is a good idea to try one first so that you don't overseason the masala. Cover and place in the fridge while you roast your papads.

Heat a dry frying pan over medium heat. With a brush or your hand, spread a little oil over a papad on both sides. Place it in the centre of the pan and press it down with a spatula. You will be able to see the papad cooking through. When this begins to happen, flip it over and press it down again with your spatula. Continue flipping until the papad is nicely roasted on both sides and cooked through. Transfer to a wire rack and continue cooking the rest of the papads in the same way.

To serve, top each papad with about 2 tablespoons of the masala.

CHANA DHAL SUNDAL

SERVES 4 AS A SNACK

This tasty South Indian snack is normally eaten by hand but feel free to dig in using a spoon if you like.

PREP TIME: 5 MINS, PLUS SOAKING TIME
COOKING TIME: 12 MINS

200g (1 cup) dried chana dhal (yellow split chickpea lentils)
2 tbsp sesame oil
½ tsp black mustard seeds
2 long dried red chillies
2 fresh green chillies, split lengthwise
20 curry leaves, roughly chopped
A pinch of asafoetida*
A pinch of ground turmeric
Salt and freshly ground black pepper
Juice of 1 lemon, to serve

Soak the lentils in cold water for about 30 minutes–2 hours. Rinse them, then place in a pan and cover with fresh water. Bring the water to a boil, then reduce to a simmer. You only want to cook the lentils for about 7–10 minutes. The lentils should be soft enough to crush between two fingers but still keep their shape. Drain and set aside.

Now heat the oil in a large frying pan over medium–high heat. When visibly hot, add the mustard seeds. When they begin to crackle, add the dried red chillies, green chillies and curry leaves and temper these in the oil for about 30 seconds. Add the asafoetida and turmeric and season with salt and pepper. Stir in the drained lentils until they are all covered in the oil mixture.

To serve, squeeze the lemon juice over the top and serve hot or at room temperature.

NOTE
*If you are gluten-free, please check the asafoetida packaging as some brands of contain wheat flour.

SPICY MASALA POPCORN

SERVES 2

One thing I enjoy about going out to a good Indian restaurant is finding something new. I don't care if the dish is complicated, it just needs to be memorable, like the first time I tried masala popcorn ('gunpowder popcorn' on their menu) at Curry Leaf Cafe in Brighton. You can easily make more: as a guide, 100g (½ cup) of popcorn kernels will serve two – just be sure to increase the spiced butter too. For ease, you could use microwave popcorn.

PREP TIME: 1 MIN
COOKING TIME: 6–10 MINS

2 tbsp rapeseed (canola) oil
100g (½ cup) popping corn
2–3 tbsp butter
1 tsp ground cumin
1 tsp ground coriander
1 tsp garam masala and/or chaat masala
½ tsp chilli powder
½ tsp fine sea salt
2 limes, cut into wedges, to serve

Pour the oil and popcorn kernels into a large non-stick pan with a tight-fitting lid. Coat the kernels with the oil. Cook, covered, over medium–high heat until all of the kernels have popped.

While the popcorn is cooking, melt the butter in a small saucepan. Stir in the spices and salt.

Put the popcorn in a serving bowl and pour the butter and spice mixture all over. Toss well. Serve with lime wedges and squeeze the lime juice over the popcorn to taste.

MAKE IT VEGAN

Use vegetable ghee or butter instead of dairy butter. You could also just leave it out.

PAPADDA VADA

(PAPADAMS FRIED IN A SPICY RICE BATTER)

MAKES 20 – FEEDS A CROWD

Papadams are delicious but this Keralan recipe takes them to the next level. The papads are dipped into a spicy batter before deep-frying. Unlike plain papads, these battered papads stay about the same size when fried. They are delicious served with a selection of pickles, sauces and chutneys.

PREP TIME: 10 MINS, PLUS SOAKING TIME
COOKING TIME: 20 MINS

Rapeseed (canola) oil, for deep-frying
20 papads

FOR THE BATTER
275g (1½ cups) Basmati rice, rinsed and soaked in water for 5 hours, then drained
½ tsp ground turmeric
1 tsp chilli powder
1 heaped tbsp black sesame seeds
1 tsp cumin seeds
1 tbsp dried chilli (hot pepper) flakes (optional)
½ tsp salt

To make the batter, place the soaked rice in a food processor and add just enough fresh water to blend it into a thick batter. Whisk in the rest of the ingredients. The batter should be thick enough to adhere to the papads when dipped into it. If it is too thick to easily dip, add a drop more water – it should be the consistency of double (heavy) cream.

Heat the oil in a large saucepan or wok until hot enough to deep-fry. If you drop a piece of papad into the oil and it sizzles and floats to the top immediately, the oil is ready.

Dip the first papad into the batter, ensuring that it is very well coated, and gently place it into the oil. Fry for about 40 seconds, until the batter coating turns light brown. Transfer with a slotted spoon to a wire rack over a tray or to a piece of paper towel. Allow the excess oil to drip into the pan or drain into the paper while you finish cooking the remaining papads.

Clockwise from top left:
papadda vada (see left); green coconut chutney (page 129); mango pickle (page 127); masala papads (page 13) with tomato, onion and mint salad (page 124); tajah badam (page 12); posh Bombay mix (page 12); spicy masala popcorn (left)

UZHUNNA VADA
(SAVOURY LENTIL DONUTS)

MAKES 20 – FEEDS A CROWD

I have enjoyed uzhunna vada many times over the years but they are never as good as homemade. At busy restaurants, it is difficult to fry and serve the vada immediately, which is much easier to do when cooking at home. In the UK, these crispy and fluffy fried *vada* are often served as a starter with other fried snacks but in Kerala they are usually served for breakfast, like bagels. These are delicious as a starter, but also try them as a main with my sambar and uzhunna vada combo on page 80.

PREP TIME: 10 MINS, PLUS SOAKING TIME
COOKING TIME: 8 MINS

- 300g (1½ cups) plus 1 tbsp white split urad dhal lentils
- 20 fresh curry leaves, chopped
- 3 green chillies, finely chopped
- 1 tbsp ginger paste (or equal amount of finely chopped ginger)
- 3 tbsp finely chopped coriander (cilantro)
- ½ tsp baking powder
- ½ tsp table salt
- 2 tbsp peppercorns, roughly crushed
- Rapeseed (canola) oil, for deep-frying

TO SERVE
- Mint and coriander sauce (see page 9)
- Green and/or red coconut chutney (see page 129)
- Yoghurt sauce (see page 9)

Roast the 1 tablespoon of urad dhal in a dry frying pan over medium–high heat until the lentils are nicely browned. Set aside.

Soak the rest of the urad dhal in water for 4 hours or overnight. Then place them in a food processor with about 2 tablespoons of water and blend until you have a smooth but thick batter. Whisk all the other ingredients except the oil into the batter, including the roasted lentils.

Heat about 10cm (4in) of oil in a saucepan until visibly hot. If you drop a piece of the batter into the oil and it sizzles and rises to the top immediately, you're ready to go. Place a bowl of water next to your batter, as it helps to have wet hands when forming the uzhunna vada, and rub a large metal spoon with oil to help the vada slide off. Dip a hand in the water and pick up about a half handful of the batter. Place the batter on the spoon and form it into a small ring donut shape by working your finger into the centre.

Carefully lower the vada into the oil and start forming your next uzhunna vada. Work quickly and cook in small batches of about four or five. Don't worry too much if they don't look perfect at first. You will get better at it. Allow the uzhunna vada to fry for about 3 minutes or until golden brown. They should be nice and crispy on the exterior and soft and spongy inside. Keep them warm while you make the rest.

Serve with mint and coriander sauce, green and/or red coconut chutney, yoghurt sauce or any sauce that sounds good.

BLACK BEAN AND CHEDDAR SAMOSAS

MAKES ABOUT 20

These samosas, pictured on page 20, are great with tomato salsa or coriander sauce (as per the recipe on page 9 but leaving out the mint and adding more coriander/cilantro). For ease, I recommend using ready-made samosa wrappers – available at most Asian shops in the freezer section. If you want to make your own wrappers and/or would like to watch how I fold samosas, I've made a video for you on my YouTube channel, Dan Toombs. The wrapped (but unfried) samosas can easily be frozen: simply spread out on a baking tray, transfer to a freezer bag once frozen and thaw fully before frying.

PREP TIME: 25 MINS
COOKING TIME: 20 MINS

2 tbsp rapeseed (canola) oil, plus extra for deep-frying
½ onion, finely chopped
2 garlic cloves, minced
2 x 400g (14oz) tins (cans) black beans, drained and rinsed
½ tsp chilli powder
½ tsp ground cumin
1 handful of grated Cheddar cheese
Salt
20 shop-bought rectangular samosa sheets
3 tbsp plain (all-purpose) flour

Heat the oil in a saucepan over medium–high heat. When hot, add the onion and fry for about 5 minutes, until soft and translucent. Stir in the garlic and fry for a further 30 seconds, then pour in the beans, chilli powder and ground cumin. Reduce the heat to medium and start mashing it all up with a potato masher until you have a mixture the consistency of mashed potatoes. Whisk in the cheese and add salt to taste. Allow to cool. The bean mixture will become thicker as it cools.

To make the samosas, take a samosa sheet and place it on clean surface with one of the short ends closest to you. Mix the flour with enough water to make a thick paste, ready for sealing the samosas. Take the top left corner of the samosa sheet and bring it about halfway down to meet the right-hand side. You should be able to see a perfect triangle in the pastry but the shape you create will actually be a diamond. Now fold the top right corner down to meet the left-hand side, creating a triangular pocket with a small flap. Fill the pocket with a generous tablespoon of the filling and fold the small triangular flap and pastry over to close. Now rub the flour paste all over the surface of the remaining pastry, and fold it into a neat triangle to seal. If there are any holes in the corners, use the paste to seal them too. Repeat with the rest of the samosa wrappers and filling.

Heat about 10cm (4in) of rapeseed oil in a large pan or wok to 170°C (338°F) – or until a piece of samosa sizzles immediately when dropped in the oil. You don't want to overcrowd the pan so you might need to work in batches. Fry for a couple of minutes, turning the samosas a few times as you do, until they are crisp and light brown. Keep warm while you fry any remaining batches.

NOTE

For a lighter option, brush them with a little oil and bake at 200°C (400°F/Gas 6) for 20 minutes or until heated through and browned.

MAKE IT VEGAN

These are excellent without cheese or you could use a vegan cheese.

SMOKED TOOR DHAL SAMOSAS

MAKES ABOUT 25

I tried smoked toor dhal samosas at a little street food stall in Mumbai. They were so good, I had to try making them at home. Samosa pastry is available at most Asian shops in the freezer section but if you want to try making your own and/or would like to see how I fold them, watch my samosa video on my YouTube channel, Dan Toombs. To try these samosas smoked, you will need to light charcoal, as described below, or use a home smoker for an easier and smokier process. They are pictured overleaf.

PREP TIME: 1 HOUR, PLUS SOAKING AND RESTING TIME
COOKING TIME: 35 MINS

150g (1 cup) toor dhal
½ tsp salt
½ tsp ground turmeric
2 tbsp finely chopped ginger
1 tsp amchoor (dried mango powder)
1 tsp garam masala
3 tbsp finely chopped coriander (cilantro)
½ tsp rapeseed (canola) oil, plus extra for deep-frying
25 shop-bought rectangular samosa sheets
Your favourite chutneys, to serve
Lime wedges, to serve

FOR THE TEMPERING
2 tbsp rapeseed (canola) oil
1 tsp mustard seeds
1 tsp cumin seeds
2 green chillies, finely chopped
10 curry leaves, roughly chopped

Rinse the dhal several times, cover with water and soak for 30 minutes.

Meanwhile, light a few pieces of lump wood charcoal outside to become white-hot (optional).

Pour the lentils into a pan with the salt, turmeric and ginger and cover with 1 litre (4 cups) water. Bring to a boil over high heat, then reduce the heat and simmer for 30 minutes, or until the dhal is really soft. Stir in the amchoor (dried mango powder) and garam masala. You want the dhal to be really thick as it is a stuffing, so reduce the water down until good and thick. Stir regularly so it doesn't burn to the bottom of the pan. Set aside to cool; it will thicken more as it does.

Now heat the tempering oil over high heat in another pan until visibly hot. When hot, add the mustard seeds. When they begin to pop, reduce the heat to medium and stir in the cumin seeds, chillies and curry leaves. Temper for about 40 seconds, then pour it over the cooked dhal and whisk it in, along with the coriander (cilantro).

By this time, your charcoal should be ready. Using tongs, place the hot charcoal on a piece of foil and carefully transfer to the pan with the dhal. Drizzle the ½ tsp of rapeseed (canola) oil over the charcoal – it will begin to smoke heavily. Cover the pan and let the dhal smoke until all the smoke is gone. I normally smoke mine in my Traeger or smoker, which I find more convenient. Feel free to use a smoker if you have one.

Take a samosa sheet and wrap the filling up as explained on page 18. Repeat with the rest of the samosa wrappers and filling.

When all of your samosas are wrapped, you can freeze them if you wish. Spread them out on a baking tray and then transfer to a freezer bag once frozen. Be sure to thaw them first before frying.

If frying immediately, heat about 10cm (4in) oil in a large pan or wok to 170°C (338°F) and fry in batches for about 3 minutes, until crispy and lightly browned. Keep warm while you fry the remaining samosas.

Serve with your favourite chutneys and lime wedges for squeezing.

NOTE

For a lighter option, preheat your oven to 200°C (400°F/Gas 6), brush each samosa with a little oil and bake for about 20 minutes or until heated through and browned to your liking.

Top plate: samosa pinwheels (see right); smoked toor dhal samosas (page 19); tomato, onion and mint salad (page 124)
Bottom chopping board: black bean and Cheddar samosas (page 18) with tomato, onion and mint salad (page 124)
Left: mint and coriander sauce (page 9) and smoked toor dhal samosa (page 19)

POTATO AND ARTICHOKE SAMOSA PINWHEELS

SERVES 4 OR MORE AS PART OF A MULTI-COURSE MEAL

I'm a big fan of samosa pinwheels. Not only do they look great, they're also a lot easier to prepare than normal samosas. This potato and artichoke combo is a good one, but feel free to experiment with other fillings. The black bean samosa filling on page 18 works really well cooked this way. Unlike other samosas, these pinwheels do not freeze well so it is best to make and fry them on the same day.

PREP TIME: 30 MINS, PLUS RESTING TIME FOR THE DOUGH
COOKING TIME: 15 MINS

2 tbsp rapeseed (canola) oil or ghee
1 onion, finely chopped
2 tbsp garlic and ginger paste
2 green chillies, finely chopped
1 tsp ground cumin
1 tsp ground coriander
1 tsp garam masala
½ tsp ground turmeric
400g (14oz) mashed potato (about one large potato)
200g (7oz) cooked artichoke hearts, diced
2 tbsp lemon juice
3 tbsp chopped coriander (cilantro)
Rapeseed (canola) oil, for frying
4 heaped tbsp plain (all-purpose) flour, plus extra for dusting

FOR THE PASTRY
150g (heaped 1 cup) plain (all-purpose) flour
1 tbsp rapeseed (canola) oil
1 tsp cumin seeds
½ tsp salt

TO SERVE
Mint and coriander sauce (see page 9)
Tamarind sauce (see page 10)
Yoghurt sauce (see page 9)

To make the filling, heat the oil in a large frying pan over medium–high heat. When hot, add the chopped onion and fry until soft and translucent. Stir in the garlic and ginger paste, green chillies, cumin, coriander, garam masala and turmeric. Now add the mashed potato and artichoke and stir until well combined. It should have a nice yellow glow because of the turmeric. Stir in the lemon juice and chopped coriander (cilantro) and set aside to cool.

Now make the pastry. Mix the flour, oil, cumin seeds and salt in a bowl and slowly add about 80ml (5½ tablespoons) water while working with your hands until you have a soft but dry dough. Let it sit for about 30 minutes, covered with a wet tea (dish) towel.

To make the pinwheels, roll the dough out on a lightly floured surface into a circle that is slightly thicker than a chapatti – about 20cm (8in) diameter. Spread the potato and artichoke mixture evenly all over the surface. It should look like a big potato pizza. Starting at one end, roll it into a tight cylinder, then slice into 2.5cm (1in) rounds.

When ready to cook, heat about 10cm (4in) of oil in a large wok or pan. Your oil is ready when a piece of pastry sizzles and rises to the top immediately when placed in the oil. If you have an oil thermometer, aim for 170°C (338°F).

Mix the 4 tablespoons of flour with 100ml (scant ½ cup) water in a bowl to make a thick paste.

Dip one of the pinwheels in the flour paste so it is nicely coated and carefully lower it into the oil. Repeat with the rest of the pinwheels and fry until nicely browned all over – about 3 minutes per side. You may need to work in batches to avoid overcrowding the pan. I usually turn the pinwheels over in the oil a few times for more uniform cooking. Move to paper towel to soak up excess oil, then serve with the sauces.

NOTE
For a lighter option, preheat your oven to 200°C (400°F/Gas 6), omit the flour paste and just brush each samosa pastry with a little oil, then bake for about 20 minutes or until heated through and browned to your liking.

MASALA PLANTAIN CHIPS

SERVES 4–8

Plantain chips are a popular snack and this recipe makes them extra special. The plantains can be cut into rounds, which is easiest, but if you are good with a knife or have a mandolin, try slicing them lengthwise. Doing this makes an eye-catching centrepiece. I really like the addition of the spices. Plaintains aren't really sweet like bananas, so the spices and salt complement them perfectly. Be warned, they aren't as easy as bananas to peel – I usually use a knife.

PREP TIME: 15 MINS
COOKING TIME: 15 MINS

4 green plantains
Rapeseed (canola) or coconut oil, for frying
1 tsp chilli powder
½ tsp amchoor (dried mango powder)
½ tsp garam masala or chaat masala
Salt
Your choice of chutney, to serve (optional)

Peel and slice the plantains into thin rounds, or slice them lengthwise. If you have a mandolin, use it for the slicing as it will make the slices more uniform.

Heat about 10cm (4in) of oil to 200°C (400°F). If you don't have an oil thermometer, place a couple of plantain slices in the oil when it looks like it is coming up to heat. If they sizzle immediately when placed in the oil, then it is hot enough.

Carefully add the sliced plantains to the hot oil. Be careful not to overcrowd your pan. These are not served hot so you can easily fry them in batches. Fry until golden brown in colour, about 3–4 minutes, then use a spider strainer or slotted spoon to transfer to paper towel to soak up any excess oil.

Season with the ground spices and salt to taste. Serve on their own or with a good chutney.

PAPDI
(INDIAN WHEAT FLOUR CRACKERS)

MAKES ABOUT 40 DISCS, PLUS USABLE SCRAPS

These fried or baked wheat crackers are excellent on their own as a snack but they can be and are used in lots of different ways. Try them broken up into bhel puri (see page 35); they are essentially small puris so they are amazing stirred into the bhel puri mix. You could also make dahi papdi chaat on page 32, which calls for papdi and also the three essential sauces at the beginning of this book. You could even serve them as canapés topped with whatever sounds good. You can't go wrong topping them with the tomato and onion masala used in the masala papad recipe on page 13 or soft homemade paneer (page 26). Papdis are available at Asian shops too if you would like to try one of these recipes without making them yourself.

PREP TIME: 25 MINS, PLUS RESTING TIME
COOKING TIME: 10 MINS

240g (2 cups) plain or chapatti flour, plus more for dusting
1 tsp ajwain (carom) seeds
½ tsp salt
3 tbsp melted ghee or rapeseed (canola) oil
Rapeseed (canola) oil, for deep-frying (or brushing if you are baking the papdis)
Flaky sea salt

Mix the flour with the ajwain (carom) seeds and salt, then add the melted ghee or oil. Move it around with your hands until the flour begins to look like bread crumbs. Slowly add 7 tablespoons water, 1 tablespoon at a time, and knead the flour into a firm hard dough. Cover with cling film (plastic wrap) and leave to rest for 10 minutes.

Divide the dough ball into four equal-sized balls. These will be easier to work with. Take each smaller ball and knead them for a minute or so, until you have a firm workable dough. Allow to rest, covered, for 30 minutes.

Roll out each dough ball with a heavy rolling pin until as thin as a tortilla or chapatti. Cut into small circles with a 5cm (2in) round cookie cutter. Prick each circle a couple of times with a fork. This will make them extra crispy.

Now heat about 10cm (4in) of oil in a large pan. When visibly hot, fry the papdi until they are crisp and golden brown – about 2 minutes. The oil will stop sizzling when the papdis are completely fried. Sprinkle with the flaky salt to taste and transfer the finished papdis to paper towel to drain any excess oil.

Eat immediately or allow to cool and store in an air-tight container. These will stay fresh for at least a week.

TO BAKE

Preheat your oven to 180°C (350°F/Gas 4). Brush each papdi with a little oil, place on a baking tray and bake for about 20 minutes or until golden brown in colour. They bake quickly, so keep an eye on them.

SPICY STUFFED GREEN CHILLIES

SERVES 4 OR MORE AS PART OF A MULTI-COURSE MEAL

Green chillies stuffed with spiced gram flour? You're just going to have to trust me here if you don't already know how good these are! These stuffed chillies make the perfect appetizer.

PREP TIME: 10 MINS
COOKING TIME: 10–15 MINS

125ml (½ cup) rapeseed (canola) oil
100g (heaped ¾ cup) gram (chickpea) flour
½ tsp ground turmeric
½ tsp chilli powder
½ tsp ground cumin
½ tsp ground coriander
1 tsp amchoor (dried mango powder)
Salt (I use just under 1 tsp)
350g (12oz) long green chillies
Raita or coconut chutney, to serve (optional)

Heat 1 tsp of the oil in a large frying pan over medium–high heat. Pour in the flour and work it with a whisk or fork in the pan so that it toasts evenly. The flour is ready when fragrant and lightly browned, about 2 minutes. Don't worry if you see small balls of untoasted gram flour. Break them up as best you can but any remaining are fine.

Add the turmeric, chilli powder, cumin, coriander, amchoor (dried mango powder) and salt and transfer to a mixing bowl. Pour in 70ml (4½ tablespoons) water and work with your hands into a thick paste.

Slit your green chillies down the middle and remove most of the seeds with your thumb. Stuff the chillies with the gram flour paste.

Heat the remaining oil in a frying pan over low heat. Fry the chillies until browned all over, about 2–3 minutes. You should see a few blackened spots and blisters on the chillies. Serve immediately on their own or with a good raita or coconut chutney.

(GF)

HOMEMADE PANEER WITH CHILLI, BLACK PEPPER, CUMIN AND CORIANDER

SERVES 8 OR MORE

If you just want paneer for your curries or the barbecue, shop-bought paneer will do just fine! Making paneer is a bit of a chore unless you want to do something special with it. That's what you're going to do here. As with all flavoured cheeses, you can add what sounds good but this chilli, black pepper, cumin and coriander (cilantro) combo is a good place to start. I use it in my curries but it is equally as good and eye-catching served simply as a starter with papdis (see page 23) or another cracker! You will need a good open mould to form the cheese – any shaped mould you like.

PREP TIME: 10 MINS, PLUS STANDING TIME
COOKING TIME: 10 MINS

- 1.5 litres (6 cups) whole milk
- 2–3 tbsp lemon juice
- 2 tsp dried chilli (hot pepper) flakes
- ½ tsp freshly cracked black pepper
- 2 tbsp finely chopped coriander (cilantro)
- 1 tsp cumin seeds, toasted
- 1 tsp salt (or to taste)

In a 3-litre (3-quart) saucepan, heat the milk until it is almost boiling. Be careful, as when it does boil, it will quickly bubble up and go all over your hob. So, when almost to boiling point, turn off the heat and allow to cool for a minute or two. Stir in 2 tablespoons of lemon juice. The milk will begin to curdle. Add more if necessary but you only want to use as much lemon juice as required to separate the curds and whey. Stir in the remaining ingredients.

Cover a sieve with a cheesecloth or muslin and carefully pour the curds and whey into it. The whey will run through the cloth, leaving just the curds, spices and chopped herbs behind. Wrap the cheesecloth around the curds and squeeze as much excess whey out as you can. Then tie it up and hang it on your tap to drip into the sink for 1–2 hours.

To finish, place an open mould on a clean surface and fill it with the curds. You could use a small loose-based cake tin (pan) for this, leaving the base out. Press the curds down firmly and lay something heavy on top so that it becomes compacted. You want the bottom to be open so that the cheese can continue to drain excess whey. Leave it in a cool place for a few hours, then remove your very attractive piece of paneer from the mould.

Store in the fridge and serve as is, or use it in your curries, grill it or fry it.

STREET FOOD

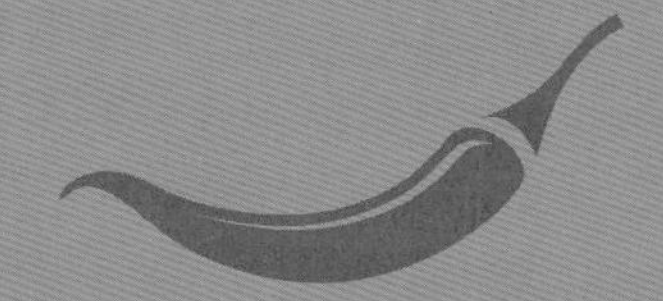

Wherever I travel, street food always seems to be what people love most. Not only is it convenient, it's real comfort food. In this chapter, I have collected some of my favourite Indian street food recipes for you. I had to give you some delicious sandwich and wrap recipes, as they are so easy to take with you and eat on the go. The chaats, however, can be a bit messy. They are normally eaten by hand, but go ahead and use some cutlery if you wish.

SAMOSA CHAAT

(SAMOSAS TOPPED WITH CHICKPEAS AND SAVOURY AND SWEET SAUCES)

SERVES 4 OR MORE AS PART OF A MULTI-COURSE MEAL

Crispy samosas right out of the hot oil take this popular chaat to a whole new level. You could use any samosas, even shop-bought, but why miss out on the fun of making them yourself? This is an excellent way to use up leftover samosas. However, your samosa chaat will be better if you make the samosas just before serving.

PREP TIME: 5 MINS, PLUS MAKING THE SAMOSAS IF USING HOMEMADE
COOKING TIME: 10 MINS

8 hot Samosas (see pages 18–19 or shop-bought)
400g (14oz) tinned (canned) chickpeas (garbanzo beans), drained and rinsed
1 large red onion, finely chopped
3 tbsp mint and coriander sauce (see page 9)
3 tbsp yoghurt sauce (see page 9)
3 tbsp tamarind sauce (see page 10)
2 large handfuls of fine sev or similar

Place two hot samosas in the centre of each of four serving plates. (If using shop-bought or left-over samosas, you could microwave them until hot, or better, place them in an oven preheated to 200°C/400°F/Gas 6 for about 10 minutes.) You could leave the samosas whole or break them up a bit. Cover the samosas with the chickpeas (garbanzo beans) and chopped red onion.

Top each chaat with mint and coriander sauce, yoghurt sauce and tamarind sauce.

To finish, cover generously with fine sev or something similar.

MAKE IT VEGAN

Substitute homemade dairy-free yoghurt and you're in for a treat.

CHAAT ALOO

(INDIAN POTATO SALAD)

SERVES 4 OR MORE AS PART OF A MULTI-COURSE MEAL

This creamy and delicious potato salad is perfect for indoor or alfresco dining. With potato salads it is essential that the potatoes are nice and soft, then cooled and mixed with the dressing ingredients.

PREP TIME: 10 MINS, PLUS CHILLING TIME
COOKING TIME: 20 MINS

500g (1lb 2oz) floury potatoes, such as Yukon Gold
2 tbsp rapeseed (canola) oil (optional)
200g (generous ¾ cup) plain Greek yoghurt
½ red onion, finely chopped
2 tsp chaat masala
½ tsp chilli powder
½ tsp ground cumin
Salt and freshly ground black pepper

TO SERVE

3 tbsp tamarind sauce (see page 10)
3 tbsp mint and coriander sauce (see page 9)
Pomegranate seeds
Sev

Peel the potatoes and cut into small cubes (we're talking potato-salad size), then boil in hot water until very tender. It will take about 8 minutes but don't rush this – they're ready when they're ready. Allow the potatoes to cool. If you want, you can fry them in a little oil until browned. This is optional.

Whisk the yoghurt until it becomes light and creamy. Add the rest of the dressing ingredients and stir well. Add salt and pepper to taste. To finish, add the potatoes and stir it all up. Chill in the fridge for about 30 minutes.

To serve, top the chaat aloo with tamarind sauce, mint and coriander sauce, pomegranate seeds and sev.

MAKE IT VEGAN

Use vegan yoghurt instead of the Greek yoghurt in both the main recipe and in the mint and coriander sauce recipe.

CRISPY FRIED SPINACH CHAAT

SERVES 2 OR MORE AS PART OF A MULTI-COURSE MEAL

Crispy fried spinach chaat is usually made with large palak leaves, which is a variety of spinach seen a lot in India but also available at Asian shops in the UK. I usually use baby spinach leaves, which are easier to come by, but it takes more time to prepare because of all the chopping. I tried my first fried spinach chaat at a great little restaurant in London called Thali. The delicious chaat was one of their signature dishes so, understandably, they weren't quite ready to give me their exact recipe. I have experimented a lot with this one and think I've got it pretty close to that chaat I enjoyed so much.

PREP TIME: 20 MINS
COOKING TIME: 10 MINS

250g (9oz) fresh spinach leaves, big stems removed
Rapeseed oil, for deep-frying
Salt
1 onion, finely chopped
1 tomato, diced

FOR THE BATTER
65g (½ cup) gram (chickpea) flour, plus extra if needed
2 tbsp rice flour
½ tsp ground turmeric
1–2 tbsp chilli powder
1 tsp garam masala

TO SERVE
4 tbsp mint and coriander sauce (see page 9)
4 tbsp tamarind sauce (see page 10)
4–5 tbsp yoghurt sauce (see page 9)
Fine sev

Wash and dry your spinach leaves and remove the large stems. You will be shredding the majority of the leaves but hold about 8–10 large leaves back for dipping in batter. I find that it is quicker to stack the leaves to shred them. Shred the leaves finely. If you have ever tried fried seaweed at a Chinese takeaway, that is the look you are going for with this spinach.

Heat about 10cm (4 in) of rapeseed oil in a large pan or wok for deep-frying. When a piece of spinach instantly sizzles when added to the oil, you're good to go. If you have an oil thermometer, aim for 200°C (400°F).

It is a good idea to cook the spinach in batches. Fry each batch until the leaves become darker and are beginning to turn crispy, about 1–2 minutes. Transfer to paper towel to soak up any excess oil. The shredded spinach will become crispier as it dries out.

To make the batter, whisk all of the batter ingredients in a bowl with just enough water to make a thick, smooth batter. Dip the large, whole leaves in the batter. It should coat them. If you find the batter is too runny, whisk in a little more gram flour. Fry the battered leaves in the hot oil until crispy and brown, about 1–2 minutes, then transfer to paper towel to soak up any excess oil. Season the shredded and battered spinach with salt to taste.

To finish, place a big mound of shredded spinach on two plates. Top with the chopped onion and diced tomato followed by the battered spinach leaves, then garnish generously with the sauces. To serve, top with a couple handfuls of fine sev and a little more salt if you like.

MAKE IT VEGAN
Use vegan yoghurt alternatives in the sauce recipes.

DAHI PAPDI CHAAT

(WHEAT CRACKERS WITH SAVOURY AND SWEET SAUCES)

SERVES 4

This simple chaat is very similar to the pani puri recipe featured in my cookbook *The Curry Guy Easy*. Chaats are all about taking the same ingredients, perhaps adding or omitting a couple, then coming up with a completely different taste and texture sensation. In this case, rather than using the hollow puri shells, flat papdi are used. Both are often made with the same ingredients but prepared in a different way. The flavoured water (pani) used in pani puris is omitted, giving you a drier but equally tasty snack. Get the sauces and papdi (you could use shop-bought) prepared and this popular chaat can be made in minutes.

PREP TIME: 10 MINS
COOKING TIME: 20 MINS

2 large unpeeled potatoes
32 papdi, homemade or shop-bought
1 large red onion, finely chopped
250ml (1 cup) yoghurt sauce (½ recipe quantity on page 9)
250ml (1 cup) tamarind sauce (1 recipe quantity on page 10)
250ml (1 cup) mint and coriander sauce (1 recipe quantity on page 9)

TO SERVE
Chilli powder
Chaat masala (optional)
Fine sev or similar

Bring a pan of water to a boil and simmer the potatoes until soft. The cooking time will vary depending on the size of your potatoes so they are ready when they are ready. You should be able to stick a fork in with little resistance. Transfer the potatoes to a cutting board to cool. Once cooled, peel and dice them. You should be able to bite into the potato cubes with little resistance.

Arrange eight papdi on each of four serving plates. Top each papdi with the cubed potatoes and chopped onion, and drizzle over a little of each of the yoghurt sauce, tamarind sauce and mint and coriander sauce. Don't worry about doing a neat job. Like most chaats, this is meant to look a bit sloppy.

Garnish each papdi with a sprinkling of chilli powder and a little chaat masala if you like. Remember there is already chaat masala, which contains black salt, in the yoghurt sauce so you don't want to overseason.

To finish, top each plate with a handful of fine sev. These can be eaten by hand or with a fork. Serve any remaining sauce on the side.

MAKE IT VEGAN
Use vegan yoghurt alternatives in the sauce recipes.

BHEL PURI
(PUFFED RICE SNACK WITH SAVOURY AND SWEET SAUCES)

SERVES 4

Bhel puri can be made with many different ingredients but the key ingredient is kurmure (puffed rice), which can be found in most Indian/Asian shops. This delicious snack food originates from Mumbai but is now popular all over India. So much so, it's made its way to restaurants and street food stalls here in the UK. It's so good, it's addictive, and it's super easy to make too. You want to mix the ingredients up just before serving. Once you get the idea behind bhel puri, you can adjust the recipe depending on how much you want to make and what you feel like adding. Bhel puri is traditionally served in rolled-up newspapers, but a simple bowl will do.

PREP TIME: 10 MINS
COOKING TIME: 20 MINS

1 potato, unpeeled
100g (5 cups) kurmure (puffed rice)
1 red onion, finely chopped
3 green chillies, finely chopped
125ml (½ cup) mint and coriander sauce (½ recipe quantity on page 9, or shop-bought)
6 tbsp tamarind sauce (see page 10 or shop-bought)
20g (½ cup) fine sev
5 tbsp roasted peanuts
5 tbsp Bombay mix (optional)
5 papdi (see page 23) or another crispy biscuit, broken into pieces (optional)
Juice of 1 lemon
3 tbsp finely chopped coriander (cilantro)
Salt

Bring a pot of water to a boil. When ready, add the potato and boil until fork tender. The cooking time will vary depending on the size of the potato so it's ready when it's ready. Transfer to a cutting board to cool. Then peel and cut into small cubes.

In a large bowl, mix the kurmure (puffed rice), onion, green chillies and potato together well. Add the mint and coriander sauce along with the tamarind sauce. Try to coat all of the rice with the sauces. Now stir in the remaining ingredients, season with salt and serve.

NOTE

Many other ingredients are popular additions to bhel puri. Try pomegranate seeds or finely diced mango for a good sweet touch, or broken potato crisps.

HARA BHARA KEBAB BURGER

(POTATO, SPINACH AND PANEER BURGER)

MAKES 8 BURGER-SIZED KEBABS

Hara bhara kebabs not only look great but they're also delicious and good for you. These can be eaten on their own with a little mint and coriander chutney or mango pickle, or used as a filling for the franky wrap (see page 42) or kathi roll (see page 44). I like to add small, hot hara bhara kebabs to tomato-based curries, or substitute them for the paneer in my butter paneer recipe (see page 56). Be sure to add them at the end of cooking, though, so that they don't fall apart. You really can't beat a good burger so that's how I've done them here.

PREP TIME: 15 MINS, PLUS CHILLING TIME
COOKING TIME: 25 MINS

- 1 large potato, about 350g (12oz), cut into 6 pieces
- 225g (8oz) spinach
- 5 tbsp rapeseed (canola) oil
- 3 green cardamom pods, lightly smashed
- 2.5cm (1in) cinnamon stick
- 2 cloves
- 1 tsp cumin seeds
- 1 tsp coriander seeds
- 1 small onion, finely chopped
- 30g (¼ cup) peas
- 100g (3½oz) mint
- 100g (3½oz) coriander (cilantro), finely chopped
- 2–3 green chillies, finely chopped
- 5 garlic cloves, finely chopped
- 2.5cm (1in) ginger, finely chopped
- 125g (4½oz) paneer, grated
- 2 tbsp gram (chickpea) flour, plus extra if needed
- 1 tsp chaat masala
- Juice of 1 lime
- Salt

Bring a pan of water to the boil and cook the potato for about 10 minutes, until soft. Use a slotted spoon to fish out the potato chunks, then mash them lightly with a fork.

Now blanch the spinach in the same water for about 30 seconds. Remove it from the water and squeeze as much of the water out as you can, then finely chop it.

Heat a frying pan over medium heat and add 2 tablespoons of the oil. When visibly hot, stir in the cardamom pods, cinnamon, cloves, and cumin and coriander seeds. Move the spices around in the oil for about 45 seconds, then remove the cardamom pods and cinnamon.

Add the chopped onion and fry for about 5 minutes, until translucent and soft. Stir in the blanched spinach, mashed potato, peas, mint, coriander, chillies, garlic and ginger and cook for a further 3 minutes. Allow to cool.

Place these ingredients with the paneer, gram (chickpea) flour and chaat masala in a food processor or large pestle and mortar and blend to a thick paste. Add the lime juice and salt to taste if needed.

Form this paste into 8 large patties (or you could make more smaller ones, if you wish). If you find that it is too wet, you could add a little more gram flour. Place the patties in the fridge for about 15 minutes before frying.

When ready to cook, heat the remaining oil in a frying pan and fry the patties for about 3 minutes per side or until lightly browned and heated through.

NOTE

You can substitute about 150g (5½oz) defrosted shop-bought frozen spinach for the fresh spinach if you wish. There is no need to blanch this as it was done before freezing.

MAKE IT VEGAN

You could leave the cheese out or use the non-dairy cheese of your choice. Why not top it all with some meltable dairy-free cheese?

MINI RUNNER BEAN WRAP

SERVES 4

In the summer after my first cookbook was published, I was invited by Michelin-starred chef and author Atul Kochhar to cook with him at two of his restaurants, Indian Essence and Sindhu. I'd been reading Atul's cookbooks for years so it was pretty cool to actually be cooking with him and his team. We both cooked three different dishes for the special menus and this mini runner bean wrap was Atul's starter course. This isn't his exact recipe but I think I've got it pretty close. The dish was made even more special with red beetroot homemade chapattis. You could, of course, use shop-bought chapattis, but if you would like to try making the red ones pictured opposite, I've got the recipe for you on page 138.

PREP TIME: 10 MINS
COOKING TIME: 10 MINS

3 tbsp rapeseed (canola) oil
1 tsp black mustard seeds
1 tsp cumin seeds
½ tsp white split urad dhal lentils
10 fresh curry leaves
2 tbsp garlic and ginger paste
2 green chillies, finely chopped
300g (10½oz) runner beans, roughly chopped
Salt
5 tbsp Greek yoghurt
1 tbsp Dijon mustard
1 tsp runny honey (more or less to taste)
4 hot fresh beetroot chapattis (see page 138) or shop-bought chapattis, to serve
Hot sauce of choice, to serve (optional)

Heat the oil in a large frying pan over medium–high heat. When visibly hot, add the mustard seeds. When they begin to pop, stir in the cumin seeds and urad dhal. Temper the spices and lentils in the oil for about 30 seconds, then add the curry leaves. When the curry leaves become fragrant (about 30 seconds) add the garlic and ginger paste and the chopped green chillies. Stir this all up well, then add the runner beans. Fry for about 2 minutes, then add about 5 tablespoons water. Cook until the water has almost evaporated and the beans are cooked through. Season with salt to taste and keep warm.

Whisk the yoghurt, mustard and honey together. Serve the runner beans on top of hot chapattis, drizzled with the yoghurt mixture and a little hot sauce if you like.

MAKE IT VEGAN

Leave out the yoghurt sauce and top with your favourite hot sauce, or try making the yoghurt sauce with soy or coconut vegan yoghurt.

VADA PAV

(DEEP-FRIED MILDLY SPICED POTATO BURGER)

MAKES 8

This is a delicious way to use up leftover mashed potatoes. The mashed potato is first fried with a few complementary spices and herbs, and then formed into large balls that are dipped into a seasoned gram-flour batter. Everything, right up to making the sandwich, can be done ahead of time. At busy restaurants and street stalls, the potato vada are formed and fried earlier in the day and then heated through again in hot oil before serving. This is really convenient if you are serving a group of friends. When I tried these at food stalls in India, there was always a plate of roasted chillies you could help yourself to for topping your vada pav, making them as mild or spicy as you want. If you really want to treat yourself, spread lots of butter on the buns before grilling!

PREP TIME: 10 MINS
COOKING TIME: 25 MINS

- 4 potatoes (about 800g/1lb 12oz), peeled and diced
- 3 tbsp rapeseed (canola) oil
- 1 tsp black mustard seeds
- ½ tsp ground turmeric
- 3 green chillies, finely chopped, plus more for garnish
- 1 tbsp finely chopped ginger
- 1 tsp chilli powder
- 10 curry leaves, roughly chopped
- Salt
- 3 tbsp finely chopped coriander (cilantro)
- Oil, for deep-frying

FOR THE BATTER

- 120g (1 cup) sifted gram (chickpea) flour, plus extra if needed
- ½ tsp salt
- ½ tsp chilli powder
- ½ tsp ground turmeric

TO FINISH

- 4 soft hamburger buns (pav)
- Ghee, butter or oil, for browning the buns
- Mint and coriander sauce (see page 9)
- Tamarind sauce (see page 10) (optional)
- Roasted green chillies

Boil your diced potatoes in water for about 10 minutes, until fork tender. Drain and mash.

Heat the oil in a large frying pan over medium–high heat. Add the mustard seeds. When they begin to pop, stir in the turmeric, green chillies, ginger, chilli powder and curry leaves. Move this all around in the pan to flavour the oil, then add the mashed potatoes and mix well. Season with salt to taste and add the chopped coriander (cilantro). Allow to cool slightly, then form into 8 lemon-sized balls.

Whisk the batter ingredients together, adding enough water slowly to make a thick and smooth batter. The batter should cling to and coat the vada. If you find it is too thin, sift in a little more flour.

Heat the oil for deep-frying in a large pan. The oil should be deep enough to cover the vada. You are ready to start deep-frying when a piece of potato sizzles immediately when dropped into the hot oil. If you have an oil thermometer, aim for 200°C (400°F). Carefully lower the vada into the oil and fry until crispy brown. About 3–5 minutes should do. Depending on the size of your pan, you may need to cook these in small batches of three or four.

While your vada are frying, brown your buns in another pan in some ghee, butter or oil. When toasted to your liking, spread the mint and coriander sauce over the bun halves. Place a vada on top of the bottom bun and top the vada with tamarind sauce, if using, and one or more roasted chillies if you like it spicy. Add the top bun and serve.

<30

VEGETABLE FRANKY WITH CORN KOFTAS

(SAUCY WRAP WITH CORN DUMPLINGS)

SERVES 4

This one is juicy! It might have a lot of sauce but the corn koftas can stand up to it. You could use any veggie koftas. Try the hara bhara kebab burger (see page 36) instead of the corn koftas. Or give the filling for the vada pav (see page 41) a try. The most important thing is that you wrap it all up tightly so you don't get it all on your lap! I should probably mention that when I made these corn koftas during the photoshoot for this book, they were a real hit!

PREP TIME: 10 MINS
COOKING TIME: 20 MINS

Oil, for deep-frying
Gram (chickpea) flour, for dusting
4 tortillas, chapattis or rumali rotis
Yoghurt sauce (see page 9)
Mint and coriander sauce (see page 9)
Lettuce (optional)
Sliced onions (optional)

FOR THE KOFTAS

1 large potato (about 300g/10½oz), peeled and diced
1 x 400g (14oz) tin (can) of sweetcorn (or cook 2 large corn on the cobs from fresh)
1 tsp chilli powder
1 tsp ground cumin
1 green chilli, finely chopped
3 tbsp finely chopped coriander (cilantro)
Salt

To make the koftas, boil your diced potato in water for about 10 minutes, until fork tender. Drain and mash.

Pound the corn in a pestle and mortar into a paste. Mix the corn and mashed potato with the chilli powder, cumin, green chilli and coriander (cilantro). Season with salt to taste and form the mixture into short sausage shapes or small ball shapes.

Heat about 10cm (4in) oil in a wok or large pan to 170°C (338°F). If you don't have an oil thermometer, drop a piece of the corn mixture in the oil. If it sizzles and rises to the top immediately, you're ready to cook. When it reaches this heat, dust a kofta in the gram (chickpea) flour and place it in the oil. Repeat with the rest. (You may need to cook them in batches, depending on the size of your pan.) The koftas are ready once nicely browned and heated through, about 3 minutes.

To finish, smother the tortillas with a good dose of yoghurt sauce and mint and coriander sauce and divide the koftas between them. If you like, you could also add some lettuce, sliced onions or whatever you want. Then wrap it all up to serve.

MAKE IT VEGAN

Use vegan yoghurt alternatives in the sauce recipes.

PANEER KATHI ROLL

SERVES 4

This is a different way of making paneer kathi rolls. Usually the paneer is cubed and then wrapped in a chapatti. This is very good, but I like the paneer grated, as I saw it done at Zindiya Streatery and Bar in Birmingham. The cheese is heated through and mixed well with all the other ingredients, making the plain old paneer kathi roll a luxurious and mouth-watering wrap.

PREP TIME: 10 MINS, PLUS OVERNIGHT SOAKING THE DHAL
COOKING TIME: 10 MINS

4 chapattis or parathas (shop-bought or homemade), warmed
Mint and coriander sauce (see page 9)
Tamarind sauce (see page 10)

FOR THE SALAD
4 tbsp washed moong dhal, soaked in water overnight
150g (5½oz) red cabbage, finely shredded
150g (5½oz) white cabbage, finely shredded
1 red onion, diced
1 carrot, grated
2 tbsp extra virgin olive oil
Juice of 1–2 limes
Salt and freshly ground black pepper

FOR THE FILLING
2 tbsp rapeseed (canola) oil
1 tsp black mustard seeds
2 dried red Kashmiri chillies, broken into 3 pieces and deseeded
1 onion, finely chopped
½ tsp ground turmeric
200g (7oz) paneer cheese, grated

Start by mixing the salad. Toss all the ingredients in a large bowl and season to taste. Cover and place in the fridge until ready to use.

For the filling, heat the oil in a large frying pan over medium–high heat. When visibly hot, add the mustard seeds. When they begin to pop, add the Kashmiri chillies, followed by the chopped onion. Allow the onion to fry until translucent and lightly browned – about 5 minutes should do it. Now stir the turmeric into the oil, then add the grated cheese. Stir this around until it is heated through.

Divide the cheese mixture between 4 warmed chapattis. Top with equal amounts of the salad and top with the mint and coriander and tamarind sauces. Wrap tightly, then cut each kathi in half diagonally. Serve immediately.

MAKE IT VEGAN
These wraps are delicious even without the grated paneer. You could simply leave the paneer out or choose your favourite dairy-free cheese. I have used both non-dairy grated mozzarella and Cheddar with good results.

MUMBAI TOASTIE

SERVES 2

If you haven't tried the famous Mumbai toastie yet, it's time you did. These are so good. Buttered fluffy white bread topped with seasoned potatoes, vegetables and the essential mint and coriander sauce... this is a sandwich you would expect from the exciting city that is Mumbai. These are often served as a simple sandwich, but for me, it's the buttered and toasted version that gets it! If you've made some of my potato curry (see page 74) or the beetroot and potato masala dosas (page 86) and have leftovers, you could use either of these potato preparations on these toasties if you wish.

PREP TIME: 10 MINS
COOKING TIME: 20 MINS

FOR THE POTATO FILLING

- 2–3 tbsp ghee or vegetable ghee
- 1 tsp cumin seeds
- 10 curry leaves
- 1 onion, finely chopped
- 2–3 green chillies, sliced into rings
- ½ tsp ground turmeric
- 1 tsp chilli powder (optional)
- 1 tbsp garlic and ginger paste
- 2 potatoes, peeled and cut into cubes
- Salt and freshly ground black pepper
- 3 tbsp chopped coriander (cilantro)

TO ASSEMBLE

- 150ml (scant ⅔ cup) mint and coriander sauce (page 9) but without the yoghurt
- 4 pieces of white bread
- 4 slices of Cheddar cheese
- 8 slices of tomato
- 8 slices of cucumber
- 8 slices of red (bell) pepper
- 8 slices of red onion
- Butter, for frying

To make the potato filling, heat the ghee in a large pan over medium–high heat. When hot, add the cumin seeds and curry leaves. Temper these in the hot oil for about 30 seconds and then add the chopped onion. Fry for about 5 minutes, until fragrant and soft, then add the chillies, turmeric, chilli powder (if using) and garlic and ginger paste. Stir this all up well and tip in the cubed potatoes. Add just enough water to cover and simmer until the potatoes are fork tender and quite dry – about 10 minutes should do. Season with salt and pepper to taste and stir in the chopped coriander (cilantro). Set aside to cool slightly.

When ready to make the toastie, spread the coriander and mint sauce all over each slice of bread. Top two of the slices of the bread with the potato mixture, spreading it evenly all over the bread. Then stack each of these slices with 2 pieces of cheese, 4 tomato slices, 4 cucumber slices, 4 (bell) pepper slices and 4 slices of red onion. Place these pieces of bread on top.

Heat a large frying pan over medium–high heat. Add a good couple of tablespoons butter and fry the sandwiches in the butter. When nicely browned, carefully flip them over and fry the other side until browned. Serve immediately.

MAKE IT VEGAN

Use vegetable ghee instead of the butter, and use a good vegan meltable cheese instead of the Cheddar. Omit the mayonnaise.

KOTTU ROTI

(VEGETABLE CURRY WITH EGGS AND PARATHAS)

SERVES 4 OR MORE AS PART OF A MULTI-COURSE MEAL

This is Sri Lankan street food at its best. It's so good, restaurants here in the UK have started serving it too. I've often seen it made by chefs and love how they really get into their work, using two sharp handheld choppers to cut everything up good and small into one big saucy combo of colourful and tasty ingredients. It might look a bit of a mess but it sure is delicious. The sauce for this one is the curry of your choice, although I don't recommend using creamy curries. You can either make a fresh curry or use up your leftovers. It's a great way to give leftover curries new life. Don't use a non-stick pan for this one as the required chopping will ruin your pan.

PREP TIME: 10 MINS, PLUS MAKING THE CURRY
COOKING TIME: 15 MINS

- 3 tbsp coconut oil or rapeseed (canola) oil
- 1 large onion, thinly sliced
- 2 green chillies, finely chopped
- 1 red (bell) pepper), thinly sliced
- 2 handfuls shredded cabbage
- 1 large tomato, diced
- 2 large eggs
- 2 tbsp garlic and ginger paste
- 1 tbsp garam masala
- 3 pan-fried parathas (see page 132, or shop-bought are fine)
- 1–2 big ladles of the curry of your choice
- 3 tbsp light soy sauce (optional)
- Salt

Heat the oil in a large metal-based or cast-iron pan over medium–high heat. When visibly hot, toss in the sliced onion, chillies and (bell) pepper and fry for about 5 minutes, until the onion is soft and translucent. Add the shredded cabbage and tomato and stir it all up.

Now add the eggs, garlic and ginger paste and garam masala, and top with the fried parathas. Give it all a good stir and chop continuously with a chopper or knife until all of the ingredients are chopped small and blended well together. That's the traditional way of doing it but, of course, you could just shred everything before you start. I prefer to do it the more authentic way with a couple of handheld choppers. It's more fun.

Add a couple ladles of the curry of your choice and stir it all together. To finish, pour in the soy sauce (if using) and check for seasoning. Serve in warmed bowls.

MAKE IT VEGAN

Just omit the eggs.

CURRIES

One of the great things about good curry sauces is that they are so versatile. I have chosen and developed these curries to be prepared just as suggested or for use with other main ingredients.

I change my recipes all the time. Not on purpose, I just do. It's my hope that you will try these recipes and adjust them to your liking. There are no rules here. A mild vegetable curry could be a super spicy curry instead just by adding more fresh chillies or chilli powder. You can also add different main ingredients to the sauces. Try stirring a few small hara bhara kebabs (see page 36) or corn koftas (see page 42) into your favourite sauce. If you love tofu, substitute it for paneer – you'll get a completely different curry but it should be up your street. Just go for it and enjoy!

TINDA MASALA
(SPICY INDIAN SQUASH CURRY)

SERVES 4 OR MORE AS PART OF A MULTI-COURSE MEAL

You probably won't find tindas in your local supermarket. This is a delicious gourd that is usually available at Indian grocers. Do try to find tindas if you can. They are really good and different too. If you can't find them, you could use butternut squash cut into cubes. It won't be the same but is still very good. You can see a photo of my tinda masala on page 126; it's the spicy-looking dish next to the rice.

PREP TIME: 15 MINS
COOKING TIME: 40 MINS

10 tindas, about 500g (1lb 2oz)
2 tbsp rapeseed (canola) oil
1 tsp cumin seeds
3 tbsp snipped coriander (cilantro) stalks
1 onion, finely chopped
2 garlic cloves, finely sliced
1 tbsp garlic and ginger paste
2 green chillies
400g (14oz) tinned (canned) chopped tomatoes
½ tsp ground turmeric
½ tsp chilli powder
1 tsp ground cumin (or to taste)
1 tsp ground coriander
Salt
Juice of 1 lemon
½ tsp garam masala
3 tbsp chopped coriander (cilantro), to serve

Wash and peel the tindas and cut them into small pieces. Some chefs just quarter them but I prefer to cut them into much smaller pieces. Remove any big seeds and discard them. Set aside.

Heat the oil in a large frying pan over medium–high heat. When visibly hot, stir in the cumin seeds and temper them in the oil for about 30 seconds. Now add the coriander (cilantro) stalks, followed by the chopped onion. Fry the onion for about 5 minutes, until translucent and soft and just lightly browned.

Add the sliced garlic cloves, the garlic and ginger paste and the chillies and fry for a further minute or so. Then add the chopped tomatoes. Stir well, then add the turmeric, chilli powder, and the ground cumin and coriander. Now add the chopped tindas and pour in just enough water to cover. Bring this to a simmer. The tindas do take some time to cook through, which is why I cut mine smaller for faster cooking. Add more water to the curry as required until the tindas are fork tender. Don't rush this. Plan on about 20–30 minutes.

When the tindas are good and tender, add salt to taste and squeeze in the lemon juice. Check for seasoning, then sprinkle the garam masala over the top. Garnish with fresh coriander to serve.

CREAMY VEGETABLE KORMA

SERVES 4 OR MORE AS PART OF A MULTI-COURSE MEAL

This might look similar to the mild kormas you find at curry houses but British kormas are kormas in name only. This authentic dish is on the spicy side but the spice level can be adjusted to taste.

PREP TIME: 10 MINS
COOKING TIME: 20 MINS

1 potato, about 185g (6½oz), cut into small cubes
12 cauliflower and/or broccoli florets
75g (½ cup) peas
75g (½ cup) sweetcorn
1 carrot, peeled, finely chopped
15 green beans, roughly chopped
1 small red (bell) pepper, roughly chopped
A pinch of saffron (optional)
3 tbsp warm milk (optional)
3 tbsp ghee, clarified butter or rapeseed (canola) oil
1 cinnamon stick
3 green cardamom pods, bruised
15 fresh curry leaves
2 onions, finely chopped
1 tbsp garlic and ginger paste
3 tomatoes, diced
½ tsp turmeric
125ml (½ cup) double (heavy) cream or whisked plain yoghurt
Salt
3 tbsp finely chopped coriander (cilantro) or whole coriander leaves, to serve
1 tsp garam masala, to sprinkle

FOR THE KORMA PASTE
2 tbsp chana dhal
1 tbsp cumin seeds
1 tbsp coriander seeds
200g (generous ¾ cup) thick coconut milk or creamed coconut
30 cashews
2 tbsp sesame seeds
4 cloves
2 green chillies, roughly chopped
2 dried red chillies
1 tbsp sugar
10 black peppercorns

Parboil your cubed potato until almost cooked through. Then add the rest of the vegetables and simmer them with the potato until just cooked through but still quite fresh looking. Drain and set aside.

To make the korma paste, lightly toast the chana lentils in a dry frying pan until light brown, 1½–2 minutes, then transfer to a plate to cool. Roast the cumin and coriander seeds in the same way. They are ready when fragrant. If they begin to smoke, get them off the heat. Place the lentils, cumin seeds and coriander seeds in a spice grinder with the other paste ingredients and grind to a smooth, thick paste.

When you're ready to make the curry, soak the saffron in 3 tablespoons of warm milk (if using) and set aside. Heat the ghee, butter or oil in a large saucepan that has a lid. When visibly hot, add the cinnamon stick and cardamom pods and temper these spices in the oil for about 30 seconds before adding the curry leaves. Temper the leaves for another 30 seconds, then add the chopped onions. Fry the onions until soft and lightly browned, about 5 minutes, and then stir in the garlic and ginger paste.

Add the chopped tomatoes and turmeric and let this mixture all cook for another couple of minutes before adding your prepared korma paste. Toss in the par-cooked vegetables and about 250ml (1 cup) water to cover. Stir well and place the lid on the top. Cook, covered, for a couple of minutes, until the sauce has thickened and the vegetables are fully cooked. If you prefer a thicker sauce, remove the pan lid for a minute or until you are happy with the consistency.

Pour in the cream or yoghurt and the saffron-infused milk (if using) and cook for another 1 minute with the lid on.

To finish, season with salt to taste, garnish with the coriander (cilantro) and sprinkle the garam masala over the top.

MAKE IT VEGAN

Substitute more thick coconut milk for the cream or try substituting vegan coconut yoghurt or non-dairy cream.

BLACK-EYED BEAN CURRY

SERVES 4 OR MORE AS PART OF A MULTI-COURSE MEAL

I learned this recipe at a brilliant restaurant in Newcastle called Ury. I was invited there one afternoon to watch the head chef prepare this and a cabbage thoran (see page 118). Talk about gorgeous! This one is so easy to make but the flavours are still complex and work so well together.

PREP TIME: 10 MINS
COOKING TIME: 20 MINS

2 tbsp coconut or rapeseed (canola) oil
1 tsp brown mustard seeds
1 tsp fenugreek (methi) seeds
20 fresh or frozen curry leaves
2 onions, sliced and cut into 2.5cm (1in) pieces
2 green chillies, split lengthwise
6 garlic cloves, sliced
2.5cm (1in) ginger, peeled and julienned
1 tsp ground turmeric
½ tsp chilli powder
1 tsp ground coriander
3 tomatoes, diced, or 300–400g (10½–14oz) tinned (canned) chopped tomatoes
600g (1lb 5oz) cooked or drained, tinned (canned) black-eyed beans
200g (generous ¾ cup) plain yoghurt
4 tbsp finely chopped coriander (cilantro), to serve
Yoghurt sauce (see page 9) or extra plain yoghurt, to serve (optional)

Heat the oil in a wok or large frying pan over medium–high heat. When hot, stir in the mustard seeds. They will begin to pop. When they do, stir in the fenugreek (methi) seeds and curry leaves and temper in the oil for about 30 seconds.

Add the chopped onions and sliced green chillies and stir it all into the oil. You want to cook the onions for about 10 minutes, until they are good and soft and lightly browned. Stir in the garlic and ginger. Sprinkle in the turmeric, chilli powder and ground coriander. Add the diced tomatoes, or if you prefer a deeper colour, try adding some tinned (canned) tomatoes. Give it all a good stir, then add the black-eyed beans. I normally soak and cook dried beans but tinned (canned) are a lot more convenient and work really well.

To finish, stir in the yoghurt 1 tablespoon at a time.

Serve immediately, garnished with coriander (cilantro) and a little more yoghurt or yoghurt sauce if you like.

MAKE IT VEGAN

Substitute 200ml (generous ¾ cup) thick coconut milk, or vegan coconut yoghurt, for the dairy yoghurt.

BUTTER PANEER

SERVES 4 OR MORE AS PART OF A MULTI-COURSE MEAL

Butter paneer just plain gets it! This one is so good simply served with plain white rice. This sauce isn't only good with paneer. Try making small hara bhara (see page 36) or corn kofta (see page 42) and deep-frying them before adding them to the sauce. Just wonderful!

PREP TIME: 15 MINS, PLUS MARINATING TIME
COOKING TIME: 20 MINS

400g (14oz) paneer, cut into 2.5cm (1in) cubes
2 x 400g (14oz) tins (cans) chopped tomatoes
2 tbsp garlic and ginger paste
4 green cardamom pods
2 cloves
1 bay leaf
1 tbsp chilli powder
2 tbsp rapeseed (canola) oil
2 green chillies, split lengthwise (optional)
80g (5½ tbsp) butter, diced
75ml (5 tbsp) single (light) cream
Salt
1½ tbsp sugar (or to taste, optional)

FOR THE MARINADE
1 tbsp rapeseed (canola) oil
2 tbsp garlic and ginger paste
1½ tsp salt
Juice of 1 lemon
2 tsp red chilli powder
120g (½ cup) Greek-style yoghurt
¼ tsp garam masala

TO SERVE
¼ tsp garam masala
2 tsp dried fenugreek leaves (kasoori methi), crushed
3 tbsp chopped coriander (cilantro)

Mix the marinade ingredients and marinate the cubed paneer for about 20 minutes.

Meanwhile, place the tomatoes, garlic and ginger paste, cardamom pods, cloves, bay leaf and chilli powder in a blender and blend until smooth. Pour this through a sieve, pressing the sauce through into an awaiting saucepan. Discard any solids that don't make it through the sieve. Bring the sauce to a low simmer and continue cooking while you prepare the paneer.

Heat the oil in a large frying pan over medium–high heat. When visibly hot, add the paneer cubes, leaving as much of the marinade in the bowl as possible. Fry the paneer on one side and then flip over to sear the opposite side. The paneer can now be used in the curry, but if time permits, go ahead and fry every side of the paneer cubes until lightly browned and crisp. Set aside.

Returning to your simmering sauce, add the chillies (if using) and stir in the butter 1 tablespoon at a time, whisking until it is emulsified into the sauce. Stir in the cream and add salt to taste. Taste the sauce. If you prefer a sweeter sauce, add about 1½ tablespoons sugar, or to taste.

To serve, whisk the reserved marinade into the sauce, 1 tablespoon at a time. Add the paneer and dust the top with the garam masala and crushed dried fenugreek leaves (kasoori methi) and sprinkle with chopped coriander (cilantro).

BALTI DHAL FRY

SERVES 2 OR MORE AS PART OF A MULTI-COURSE MEAL

This recipe is a Balti so I only cook it to serve one or two people. Authentic British Baltis are cooked in a stainless steel Balti pan over a high heat and then served in the same pan it was cooked in. That's how I hope you serve it too. There's just something about dipping fresh naans into a flaming hot Balti pan laden with delicious sizzling curry. If you don't have a Balti pan, do make this anyway! The recipe calls for a cup of cooked chana dhal. I always make a good-sized batch for ease, following the cooking instructions on the bag and freezing any leftovers, however if you just want to make enough for this recipe you will need to soak and cook 100g (½ cup) chana dhal as the lentils double in weight and size when cooked.

PREP TIME: 10 MINS, PLUS DHAL COOKING TIME IF USING HOME-COOKED
COOKING TIME: 10 MINS

- 2 tbsp coconut oil
- 2 cloves
- 2.5cm (1in) cinnamon stick
- ½ onion, very finely chopped
- 2 green chillies, finely chopped
- 1 large tomato, diced
- 2 tsp chopped coriander (cilantro) stalks
- 3–4 garlic cloves, chopped
- 1 tsp chilli powder
- ½ tsp ground turmeric
- ½ tsp ground cumin
- ½ tsp ground coriander
- 200g (1 cup) cooked chana dhal
- Salt and freshly ground black pepper
- Coriander (cilantro), to serve (optional)

FOR THE TARKA

- 2 tbsp ghee, vegetable ghee or rapeseed (canola) oil
- 3 dried Kashmiri chillies
- 1 tsp cumin seeds
- A pinch of asafoetida*

Melt the coconut oil in a saucepan over high heat. When it is good and hot, stir in the cloves and cinnamon stick. Let the spices temper into the oil for about 30 seconds and then add the chopped onion. Fry for about 2 minutes, then add the green chillies. Stir well and add the tomato and coriander (cilantro) stalks followed by the garlic and ground spices. Stir in the cooked lentils and simmer over low heat while you make the tarka.

Melt the ghee or oil in another pan. When visibly hot, add the Kashmiri chillies, cumin seeds and asafoetida. Allow to sizzle for about 30 seconds, then pour it all over the dhal.

Season to taste with salt and pepper, and garnish with fresh coriander, if using.

NOTE

*If you are gluten-free, please check the asafoetida packaging as some brands contain wheat flour.

CHOLE MASALA
(CHICKPEA CURRY)

SERVES 4 OR MORE AS PART OF A MULTI-COURSE MEAL

Chickpea curries are so good. Most are quick and easy dishes like this one. Here I use tinned (canned) chickpeas, but for even better results, you could soak dried chickpeas, then boil them in water with a half teaspoon of bicarbonate of soda (baking soda) until tender. You will also get a lot more for your money doing this. Any leftover chickpeas can be kept for about a week in the fridge for use in other curries, stew, chaats or salads.

PREP TIME: 15 MINS
COOKING TIME: 15 MINS

4 tbsp rapeseed (canola) oil
1 tsp cumin seeds
½ tsp ajwain (carom) seeds
4 green cardamom pods, bruised
5cm (2in) cinnamon stick
2 red onions, roughly chopped
2 tbsp garlic and ginger paste
1 tsp chilli powder (more or less to taste)
½ tsp ground turmeric
2 tsp ground cumin
1 tsp ground coriander
3 large tomatoes, diced
3 x 400g (14oz) tins (cans) chickpeas (garbanzo beans), drained
Salt

TO SERVE
½ tsp garam masala
Chopped coriander (cilantro)
Juice of 1 lemon
Finely chopped chillies (optional)
Matchstick (raw, julienned) ginger (optional)

Heat the oil in a large wok or frying pan over medium–high heat. When hot, stir in the cumin seeds, ajwain (carom) seeds, cardamom pods and cinnamon stick. Temper these whole spices in the oil for about 30 seconds, then add the chopped onions. Fry the onions for about 5 minutes, until soft and lightly browned.

Spoon in the garlic and ginger paste and sizzle for another 30 seconds before adding the ground spices and tomatoes. Give this all a good stir, then pour in the chickpeas (garbanzo beans). Stir well and add a little water if you like a bit more sauce. Simmer for about 5 minutes, then add salt to taste.

To finish, garnish with the garam masala and chopped coriander (cilantro). Squeeze the lemon juice in and serve with the optional chopped chillies and ginger if you like.

NOTE
Three 400g (14oz) tins (cans) of chickpeas will yield approximately 750g (30oz) of chickpeas. If using dried chickpeas, I would normally cook a full bag and keep whatever I don't use in the recipe for other dishes, but if you want just enough for this recipe, you will need to soak and cook about 375g (13oz) dried chickpeas.

DUM ALOO

(DEEP-FRIED POTATOES IN A SPICY YOGHURT SAUCE)

2 OR MORE AS PART OF A MULTI-COURSE MEAL

I first tried dum aloo at a friend's wedding. The catering company made it with small new potatoes and I loved it. It wasn't until years later that I tried it again. That time I was on a stag do somewhere in London. It's all a bit of a blur now, but I can remember that curry as if it was yesterday. A huge karahi was brought to our table filled with deep-fried whole potatoes in a thick red sauce. This is my version of that dish. I just wish I could remember where I had it.

PREP TIME: 20 MINS, PLUS SOAKING TIME
COOKING TIME: 25 MINS

- 5–6 medium roasting potatoes, peeled
- 2 tbsp rapeseed (canola) oil, plus extra for deep-frying
- 8–12 dried Kashmiri chillies, soaked in 250ml (1 cup) water for 30 mins
- 1 tbsp tandoori masala
- ½ tsp ground ginger (optional)
- 250g (1 cup) natural plain yoghurt
- 2.5cm (1in) cinnamon stick
- ½ tsp asafoetida (please be aware that some brands may contain gluten)
- 1 tsp chilli powder, plus more to taste
- 1 bay leaf
- 5 cardamom pods, bruised
- 1 tbsp fennel seeds
- ½ tsp ground turmeric
- ½ tsp ground cloves
- 1 tsp ground cumin
- 1 tsp ground coriander
- Salt and freshly ground black pepper

TO SERVE

- 3 tbsp finely chopped coriander (cilantro)
- ½ tsp garam masala
- Juice of ½ lemon

Par-cook the whole potatoes in boiling water until about 80% cooked through – about 15–20 minutes. They should be soft enough to easily stick a fork in but hard enough that you wouldn't want to start eating.

For deep-frying, heat about 10cm (4in) of oil – enough to cover the potatoes. When hot (if you have an oil thermometer, aim for 190°C/375°F), carefully place the par-cooked potatoes in the oil and fry for about 3 minutes, until crispy and brown. Set aside.

Now pour your soaked chillies and the soaking water into a blender and add the tandoori masala and ground ginger and blend until smooth. Stir this into the yoghurt in a large mixing bowl. Set aside.

To cook the curry, heat the 2 tablespoons of rapeseed (canola) oil in a large wok or frying pan over medium–high heat. Stir in the cinnamon stick, asafoetida, chilli powder, bay leaf, cardamom pods, fennel seeds, turmeric, cloves, cumin and coriander and fry it all, stirring continuously, for about 1 minute.

Now pour in the yoghurt mixture and whisk. The oil will rise to the top as it is added, so you need to whisk briskly to emulsify it into the sauce. Once you've achieved a smooth, red, emulsified sauce, add salt to taste and try it. I usually add more chilli powder at this point too as the potatoes can stand up to a spicier sauce.

In go the fried potatoes! Stir them into the sauce, then cover the pan to simmer for about 10 minutes. It's really hard to overcook a potato so just let them simmer in the sauce and become fall-about gorgeous. Cooked to perfection, you should be able to cut into them with a fork and take a sneaky bite or two. Just don't rush things. Your curry is ready when the potatoes are super soft and the sauce has thickened. Check for seasoning.

To serve, sprinkle with chopped coriander (cilantro) and garam masala and add a twist or two of lemon juice.

MAKE IT VEGAN

Substitute soy or coconut yoghurt for the dairy yoghurt. The yoghurt is used as a sauce thickener so whisking in about 1 generous teaspoon of cornflour (cornstarch) will help achieve a similar consistency.

MIXED VEGETABLE AND PANEER SABZI

SERVES 4 OR MORE AS PART OF A MULTI-COURSE MEAL.

To make this curry even nicer, run the smooth, blended sauce through a sieve, pressing all the solids through, before adding the butter. This produces a silky smooth sauce that goes so well with the vegetables and paneer. That is optional though! This one is good just as it is. I really like the green and white appearance of the dish.

PREP TIME: 10 MINS
COOKING TIME: 20 MINS

4 tbsp rapeseed (canola) oil
2 onions, finely sliced and cut into 2.5cm (1in) pieces
2 tbsp garlic and ginger paste
3 large diced tomatoes, or 400g (14oz) tinned (canned)
10 raw cashews, blended or pounded into a paste with a little water
5 handfuls (about 250g/9oz) fresh chopped spinach
50g (3½ tbsp) unsalted butter, cut into small pieces
100g (3½oz) paneer, cut into small cubes
1 potato, (about 70g/2½oz) diced into 1.25cm (½in) pieces
2 green chillies, finely chopped
100g (3½oz) cauliflower, cut into small florets
100g (3½oz) green beans, cut into 2.5cm (1in) pieces
50g (⅓ cup) peas
1 tbsp chilli powder
1 tsp ground cumin
1 tsp ground coriander
Salt
3 tbsp finely chopped coriander (cilantro), to serve
½ tsp garam masala, to serve

Heat 2 tablespoons of the oil in a large saucepan or wok over medium–high heat. When visibly hot, sauté the onions for about 5 minutes, stirring regularly, until soft and lightly browned. Stir in the garlic and ginger paste and fry for a further 30 seconds. Now pour in the tomatoes and cashew paste and simmer for a further 5 minutes. Next add the chopped spinach and 250ml (1 cup) water and simmer for 1 minute, then blend it all to a smooth sauce. If you have a handheld blender, it will make this job much easier; otherwise, transfer it to a food processor. Return the sauce to the pan and stir in the butter and let it melt into the sauce. Set aside.

Add the remaining oil to a frying pan and fry the cubed paneer on all sides until crispy and lightly browned. Transfer the paneer to a plate, leaving as much oil in the pan as possible.

Now add the potato and chillies and fry until lightly browned. Stir in the cauliflower and green beans and continue cooking until all the vegetables are about 80% cooked through but still quite al dente – about 3 minutes should do.

Add the peas and the ground spices and give it all a good stir. Pour all this into the smooth sauce you prepared earlier and heat it all up. Continue to cook the vegetables until they are cooked to your liking but be sure not to overcook them! I like mine to have a bit of bite to them. You might need to add a drop more water. Stir in the cubed paneer and season with salt to taste.

Serve garnished with coriander (cilantro) and garam masala.

MAKE IT VEGAN

Don't add the paneer or butter. It will still be superb! You can also get a nice buttery flavour using vegetable ghee. This is one of the few curries I've tried with tofu and, although I'm not a big tofu fan, I wasn't disappointed.

BROCCOLI CURRY

SERVES 4 OR MORE AS PART OF A MULTI-COURSE MEAL

This is probably one of the first vegetarian curries I ever posted on my blog. In India, I've seen many similar curries that are cooked with cauliflower instead. You could do that too as it's very good. For me, however, this one needs to be made with broccoli! Not just for flavour but for appearance.

PREP TIME: 10 MINS
COOKING TIME: 15 MINS

- 500g (1lb 2oz) broccoli, cut into small florets
- 3 tbsp ghee or coconut oil
- 2.5cm (1in) ginger, finely grated
- 70g (2½oz) grated fresh or frozen coconut
- 3 tbsp toasted sesame seeds
- 70g (½ cup) roasted peanuts
- 1 tsp red chilli powder
- 1 tsp ground turmeric
- 1 onion, finely chopped
- 2 green chillies, finely chopped
- 3 garlic cloves, finely chopped
- 3 tomatoes, roughly chopped
- 1 x 400ml (14oz) tin (can) coconut milk
- Salt and freshly ground black pepper
- ½ tsp garam masala
- Rice, puris or chapattis, to serve

Heat some water and steam the broccoli florets until just cooked – about 3 minutes. You should just be able to stick a fork into the side of the florets, but there should be some resistance. Set aside.

Now heat a large frying pan or wok over medium heat and add the ghee or oil. When hot, throw in the ginger, coconut, 2 tablespoons of the sesame seeds, the peanuts, chilli powder and turmeric and cook for about 3 minutes, stirring the ingredients about the pan with a spatula.

Stir in the onion and chillies and fry for about 5 minutes, until the onion is soft and translucent and just starting to brown.

Add the garlic and give it a good stir. When fragrant, add the chopped tomatoes followed by the par-cooked broccoli and coconut milk. Heat the broccoli through but try to ensure that it is tender but not at all mushy.

Add salt and pepper to taste and sprinkle with the garam masala and the remaining sesame seeds. Serve immediately with rice, puris or chapattis.

CHILLI PANEER STIR FRY

SERVES 2 OR MORE AS PART OF A MULTI-COURSE MEAL

This is a lip-smacking way to serve paneer. The sauce is sweet, savoury and just as spicy as you like it. Use your favourite hot sauce for this one. You can use less if you really don't like your sauces spicy hot. I like to roll the seared, soft paneer with the fried veggies and sauce into rumali rotis (see page 139). Of course, it's also good served as a saucy curry over plain white rice.

PREP TIME: 10 MINS
COOKING TIME: 10 MINS

3 tbsp rapeseed (canola) oil
200g (7oz) paneer, cubed
200g (7oz) mixed coloured (bell) peppers, roughly chopped
3 spring onions (scallions), roughly chopped

FOR THE SAUCE
250ml (1 cup) tomato ketchup
3 tbsp hot sauce
5 garlic cloves, finely chopped
2.5cm (1in) ginger, finely chopped
2 tbsp light soy sauce or coconut aminos
1 tbsp cornflour (cornstarch)
1 tsp black pepper
1 tsp white pepper
Salt
Plain rice or rotis, to serve

Start by preparing the sauce. Whisk all of the sauce ingredients together and set aside.

Heat the oil in a large frying pan over medium–high heat. When visibly hot, add the cubed paneer to the pan and brown on two sides. Stir in the (bell) peppers and spring onions (scallions) and fry until cooked through but still crisp, about 1–2 minutes.

Now add the prepared sauce and stir it all up nicely. Check for seasoning and serve hot with plain rice or wrapped into hot rotis.

AUBERGINE BALTI

SERVES 2 OR MORE AS PART OF A MULTI-COURSE MEAL

If you like a good Balti, try this one with my Balti dhal fry (see page 58). The two curries go so well together and they are a lot of fun to serve in the flaming hot Balti pans. In barbecue season, I omit the oil for the skin and prick the aubergine before cooking it right on the hot coals. I turn it a few times until it's cooked through. The smoky flavour you get is out of this world and perfect for this dish.

PREP TIME: 10 MINS
COOKING TIME: 30 MINS

1 aubergine (eggplant), about 300g (10½oz)
2 tbsp rapeseed (canola) oil
1 tsp cumin seeds
1 onion, finely chopped
1 green chilli, finely chopped
2 tbsp garlic and ginger paste
2 tomatoes, diced
½ tsp ground turmeric
1 tsp ground cumin
½ tsp ground coriander
½ tsp chilli powder
Salt
3 tbsp finely chopped coriander (cilantro), to serve

Preheat your oven to its highest setting. Rub the skin of the aubergine (eggplant) with about ½ tsp of the oil and place it on a roasting tray in the oven for about 20 minutes, or until the skin blackens and blisters. Transfer the aubergine to a chopping board and slice it in half lengthwise. Scoop out all the flesh. Discard the skin and cut the flesh into small cubes. Set aside.

Now heat the remaining oil in a frying pan over medium–high heat. When visibly hot, toss in the cumin seeds. Temper the cumin in the oil for about 20 seconds. Add the chopped onion and fry for about 5 minutes, until it is soft, translucent and lightly browned. Stir in the chilli and garlic and ginger paste. Fry for a further 1 minute or so, then stir in the diced tomatoes.

Add the dry spices while stirring, then add the diced aubergine. Let the aubergine cook until it is soft and most of the liquid has dried up, about 3–5 minutes. Season with salt to taste and check for seasoning.

Garnish with the chopped coriander (cilantro) and serve.

KALA CHANA CURRY

(BLACK CHICKPEA CURRY)

SERVES 4 OR MORE AS PART OF A MULTI-COURSE MEAL

When you look for kala chana in the shops, it is usually called 'yellow chana', though it is actually more brown in colour. When cooked it turns darker, which is why it is called 'black chana' on menus. You could use the easier-to-find white chickpeas (garbanzo beans) for this recipe, but I like the slightly different flavour and texture of the kala chana and the colour of the sauce. If using white chickpeas, the soaking water should be discarded rather than used in the sauce; you will need to add fresh water in the first step instead.

PREP TIME: 10 MINS, PLUS SOAKING TIME
COOKING TIME: 40 MINS

200g (1 cup) kala chana, soaked in 625ml (2½ cups) water overnight
½ tsp bicarbonate of soda (baking soda)
2 tbsp ghee or oil
1 tsp mustard seeds
10 curry leaves
½ tsp asafoetida*
1 tsp ground cumin
1 tsp ground coriander
1 tsp chilli powder
¼ tsp ground turmeric
1 onion, chopped
2 tbsp garlic and ginger paste
1–2 green chillies
2 medium tomatoes or 1 large tomato, diced
200g (generous ¾ cup) thick coconut milk
Salt
½ tsp garam masala, to serve
1 tbsp coriander (cilantro) leaves, to serve

Pour the soaked kala chana along with the soaking water and the bicarbonate of soda (baking soda) into a saucepan. Bring to a simmer over medium–high heat for about 30 minutes or until tender. Skim off any foam that rises to the top. Set aside when cooked.

Now heat the ghee or oil in a large frying pan over high heat. When visibly hot, add the mustard seeds. When they begin to pop, reduce the heat to medium and stir in the curry leaves. When these become fragrant, stir in the asafoetida, cumin, ground coriander, chilli powder and turmeric. Allow to sizzle in the oil for about 30 seconds. Add the chopped onion and fry for 5 minutes or until soft and translucent. Stir in the garlic and ginger paste and the chillies. Stir to combine, then add the diced tomatoes. Mix well and then stir in the coconut milk and the cooked kala chana with the cooking water. Allow to simmer for an additional 5 minutes or until you are happy with the consistency. Season with salt to taste.

To serve, sprinkle with the garam masala and coriander (cilantro) leaves to garnish.

NOTE

*If you are gluten-free, please check the asafoetida packaging as some brands contain wheat flour.

POTATO CURRY

SERVES 4 OR MORE AS PART OF A MULTI-COURSE MEAL

This delicious curry is usually served for breakfast in India. It's currently served for breakfast at my house almost weekly. It's the perfect way to start the day but it's pretty good any time of day really! You've probably seen this curry on a few Indian restaurant menus. It's delicious served over rice, but the more traditional way to serve it is with fresh homemade puris (see page 134). You could cube the potatoes, but I like to serve this one the way I was taught: simply boil your potatoes and break them up by hand into the spicy sauce. This gives you less uniform, different-sized chunks, which I like. If you have any left over, cook it down and spread it on a Mumbai toastie (see page 47).

PREP TIME: 10 MINS
COOKING TIME: 20 MINS

800g (1lb 12oz) medium potatoes
3 tbsp oil
2 tsp chana dhal
1 tsp white split urad dhal lentils
1 tsp mustard seeds
1 tsp cumin seeds
10 curry leaves
A pinch of asafoetida*
1 large onion, finely chopped
2.5cm (1in) ginger, finely chopped
2 tomatoes, diced
2–3 green chillies
⅓–½ tsp ground turmeric
½ tsp chilli powder
2 tsp gram (chickpea) flour whisked in about 3 tbsp water until smooth
Salt
½ tsp sugar (optional, more or less to taste)
2 tbsp chopped coriander (cilantro) leaves, to serve
Puris (see page 134) or rice, to serve

Bring a pan of water to a boil and add the potatoes. Cook for 15–20 minutes, until they are fork tender.

While the potatoes are cooking, heat the oil in a large saucepan over medium–high heat until visibly hot. Stir in the chana and urad lentils and fry until lightly browned. Add the mustard seeds. When they begin to pop, lower the temperature to medium and stir in the cumin seeds, curry leaves and asafoetida and fry for a further 30 seconds before adding the chopped onion. Fry the onion for about 5 minutes, until translucent and soft, then add the ginger, diced tomatoes and chillies. Add the turmeric and chilli powder and mix it all up.

Once the potatoes are cooked, transfer them to a cutting board to cool, then peel them.

Add the potatoes to the curry by breaking them up with your hands and stir in just enough water to cover. Simmer for about 5 minutes or until the potatoes are soft to your liking, then add the gram-flour (chickpea-flour) mixture and stir well. Season with salt to taste. Some people like this curry a little sweeter so you can add sugar to taste as well but I usually don't.

Garnish with the fresh coriander (cilantro) leaves and serve with rice or preferably puris.

NOTE

*If you are gluten-free, please check the asafoetida packaging as some brands contain wheat flour.

VEGETABLE STUFFED PAPAD ROLL CURRY

SERVES 4 OR MORE AS PART OF A MULTI-COURSE MEAL

The papad rolls can be a bit fussy to make. Don't fuss! Just do your best. They tend to come out fine in the end. You could use cutlery but I like to pick up the papad rolls and dip them into the sauce by hand. It's messy, mind! If you want to prepare ahead, you could make the sauce up to three days in advance, but frying the papad rolls and adding the extra cheese is best done just before serving. You can wrap anything you like into the papads – reduced potato curry (see page 74), for example.

PREP TIME: 20 MINS
COOKING TIME: 20 MINS

- 1 brown onion, roughly chopped
- 3 tbsp rapeseed (canola) oil
- 2 green chillies, finely chopped
- 1 tsp garam masala or curry powder
- ½ tsp ground turmeric
- 1 tsp chilli powder
- 1 tbsp garlic and ginger paste
- 1 x 400g (14oz) tin (can) chopped tomatoes, blended
- 2 tbsp single (light) cream
- 1 tbsp unsalted butter
- Salt
- 3 tbsp finely chopped coriander (cilantro), plus extra to serve

FOR THE PAPAD ROLLS

- 2 tbsp rapeseed (canola) oil, plus more for shallow frying
- 1 tsp cumin seeds
- 1 tsp fennel seeds
- 1 tbsp garlic and ginger paste
- 100g (3½oz) grated cauliflower
- 60g (2oz) grated carrot
- 60g (2oz) grated cabbage
- 50g ⅓ cup finely chopped green beans
- 200g (7oz) paneer, grated
- 6–10 papads

Start by making the curry sauce. Put the onion in a blender or food processor and blend to a paste with just a little water.

Heat the oil in a large frying pan over medium–high heat. When hot, pour in the blended onion and let it brown for about 3 minutes before adding the chillies, garam masala or curry powder, turmeric and chilli powder. Continue frying for another minute. The sauce should turn quite brown. Add the garlic and ginger paste and mix it all up well. Stir in the blended tomatoes and cream, then whisk in the butter until melted and emulsified into the sauce. Season with salt to taste and keep warm.

To make the papad rolls, heat the oil in a large frying pan. When visibly hot, toss in the cumin and fennel seeds. Temper them in the oil for about 20 seconds, until they become fragrant, then stir in the garlic and ginger paste and let it sizzle for a further 20 seconds. Pour in the grated vegetables and finely chopped green beans and fry until tender. A couple of minutes should do the trick. Add most of the grated paneer, then turn the heat off and let the mixture cool slightly.

Fill a deep plate or casserole with water and place a few papads in it. It is best if they aren't touching. Soak them for about 3 minutes, then carefully remove one from the water bath. Place it on a clean surface and then scoop about 2–3 tablespoons of the vegetable and paneer mixture just under the centre. Fold the sides in and then roll it up like a burrito or tight cylinder shape. Allow to dry a little while you do the same with the remaining papads.

Shallow-fry the papad rolls in oil until crispy all over. You will need to do this in batches, so keep them warm while you fry the remaining papads. Stir the reserved grated paneer into the sauce or sprinkle it on top. Place your papad rolls in the sauce so they are sticking out and garnish with coriander.

MAKE IT VEGAN

Non-dairy butter or ghee and cream can be substituted. You could also use dairy-free cheese instead of the paneer or simply leave it out.

KITCHARI
(RICE AND LENTIL CURRY)

SERVES 4 OR MORE AS PART OF A MULTI-COURSE MEAL

When I think kitchari, I think comfort food. The combination of rice and lentils with all those delicious spices is something my whole family enjoys, so I make it often. This dish is filling and really good for you too.

PREP TIME: 10 MINS, PLUS SOAKING TIME
COOKING TIME: 50 MINS

- 100g (½ cup) yellow split moong lentils, soaked overnight in water
- 100g (½ cup) Basmati rice, soaked for 30 mins
- 3 tbsp rapeseed (canola) oil or ghee
- ½ tsp black mustard seeds
- 2 tsp cumin seeds
- 2 tsp fennel seeds
- 5 curry leaves, roughly chopped
- ½ onion, finely chopped
- ½ tsp ground turmeric
- 1 tbsp garlic and ginger paste
- 1 litre (4 cups) unsalted vegetable stock or water, plus extra if needed
- 200ml (generous ¾ cup) thick coconut milk
- 1 handful of diced marrow or courgette (zucchini)
- 1 handful of diced broccoli
- 1 handful of diced cauliflower
- Salt
- 3 tbsp finely chopped coriander (cilantro), to serve
- Lime wedges, to serve

Rinse and drain the moong lentils. Wash the soaked rice with several changes of water until the water runs almost clear.

Heat the oil or ghee in a large saucepan that has a lid over medium–high heat. When hot, add the mustard seeds and wait for them to start popping. When they do, add the cumin seeds, fennel seeds and curry leaves. Temper all this in the oil for about 30 seconds, then pour in the chopped onion. Fry for about 5 minutes, until soft and translucent.

Now add the turmeric and garlic and ginger paste and stir it all up well. Add the lentils and rice and coat evenly with the oil mixture. Then cover with the vegetable stock or water and the coconut milk. Place the lid on the pan and bring to a boil. Reduce the heat to low and simmer it all gently for about 35–40 minutes or until the rice and lentils are cooked to your liking.

While the rice and lentils are simmering, steam the vegetables until just cooked through. They should be soft but still have a bit of bite to them. Tip the cooked vegetables into the kitchari and stir it all up. Season with salt to taste. If you prefer a runnier sauce, you might need to add a little more stock or water. For a drier kitchari, just cook it down to your preferred consistency. Be careful as the lentils will stick to the bottom of the pan, so stir regularly if you are reducing the sauce.

To serve, garnish with the chopped coriander (cilantro) and squeeze the lime wedges over the top to taste.

UZHUNNA VADA IN SAMBAR

(LENTIL DONUTS SERVED IN SAMBAR)

SERVES 4–6

The sambar that is used as a sauce in this dish could also be served as a sambar on its own with dosas and idlis. In this recipe, you add uzhunna vada to the sambar, which is a very popular way of eating uzhunna vada. If you happen to have uzhunna vada left over from another meal, this will give them a whole new and delicious life.

PREP TIME: 15 MINS, PLUS SOAKING TIME AND MAKING THE VADA
COOKING TIME: 1 HOUR

225g (1 generous cup) toor dhal
200ml (generous ¾ cup) thick coconut milk
150g (5½oz) chopped fresh or tinned (canned) tomatoes
8 uzhunna vada (see page 16), soaked in water for 10 mins

FOR THE SAMBAR POWDER
4 tbsp coriander seeds
2 tbsp toor dhal
2 tbsp chana dhal
1 tbsp white split urad dhal lentils
1 tbsp black peppercorns
3 tbsp Basmati rice
1 tbsp cumin seeds
1 tsp fenugreek seeds
1 tsp black mustard seeds
6 dried Kashmiri chillies
30 curry leaves, washed and dried

FOR THE TARKA
4 tbsp rapeseed (canola) oil
1 tsp black mustard seeds
½ tsp asafoetida*
1 tsp cumin seeds
10 curry leaves
75g (2½oz) aubergine (eggplant), cubed
75g (2½oz) carrot, cubed
2 green chilli peppers, finely chopped
1 red onion, finely chopped
1 tbsp tamarind concentrate
1 tbsp garlic and ginger paste (optional)
3 tbsp chopped coriander (cilantro) leaves

Rinse and soak the toor dhal in water for 20 minutes.

While the lentils are soaking, make the sambar powder. Heat a dry frying pan over medium–high heat. Add all the sambar powder ingredients and roast, stirring often, for about 1 minute, until warm to the touch and fragrant. Transfer to a plate to cool slightly, then grind to a fine powder. Set aside.

Drain the lentils and put them in a large saucepan. Add 1½ litres (6 cups) of water and simmer for about 30 minutes, until the lentils are soft. Skim off any foam that rises to the top. When the lentils are ready, stir in the prepared sambar powder, coconut milk and chopped tomatoes. If you prefer a smoother sambar, you can blend it, but this is optional.

To make the tarka, in a different pan, heat the rapeseed (canola) oil over medium–high heat. When visibly hot, add the mustard seeds. When the seeds begin to crackle, stir in the asafoetida, cumin seeds and curry leaves and temper then for about 30 seconds before adding the rest of the tarka ingredients. Fry for a further couple of minutes and then pour the tarka into the lentil mixture.

Stir and simmer until the vegetables are cooked to your liking. I prefer them to be a bit al dente, which only takes a few minutes.

To finish, add the soaked uzhunna vada and serve immediately.

NOTE

*If you are gluten-free, please check the asafoetida packaging as some brands contain wheat flour.

GOAN ROS OMELETTE
(OMELETTE WITH A RICH VEGETABLE GRAVY)

SERVES 1–2

This is a simple dish to make and really good too. Just because it's an omelette, don't think you need to serve this at breakfast time! It's good any time of day. The word 'ros' means gravy, so you're getting a delicious omelette that is smothered in a tasty, rich gravy. I tried quite a few the last time I was in Goa, both at our hotel and also from the street stalls. I've yet to have a bad one. The gravy used was different at every place we ate. This recipe makes plenty of gravy, so if serving a crowd, just increase the number of eggs used. The sauce is also good with rice or rotis.

PREP TIME: 10 MINS
COOKING TIME: 20 MINS

FOR THE GRAVY (ROS)

2 tbsp coconut or rapeseed (canola) oil
2 medium onions, finely chopped
2 tbsp garlic and ginger paste
½ tsp ground turmeric
½ tsp chilli powder (more or less to taste)
½ tsp ground cumin
400g (14oz) tin (can) of chopped tomatoes
80ml (⅓ cup) thick coconut milk
½ tsp tamarind concentrate (optional)
Salt and freshly ground black pepper

FOR THE OMELETTE

2 eggs
1 tbsp milk
1–2 green chillies, finely chopped
2 tbsp finely chopped coriander (cilantro)
Salt and freshly ground black pepper
1 tbsp unsalted butter
20g (¼ cup) grated Cheddar cheese (optional)

TO SERVE

1 tsp chopped coriander (cilantro)
1 tsp finely chopped mint leaves
½ tsp garam masala

Start by making the gravy. Heat the oil in a saucepan over medium–high heat. When visibly hot, add the onions and fry for about 5 minutes, until soft and translucent. Stir in the garlic and ginger paste and fry for a further 30 seconds. Add the turmeric, chilli powder and ground cumin and stir it all well.

Now add the tomatoes, coconut milk and tangy tamarind concentrate (if using). Top up with 250ml (1 cup) of water. Cover the pan and allow to simmer for about 10 minutes.

Meanwhile, make the omelette. Whisk the eggs and milk until creamy smooth. Add the green chillies, coriander (cilantro) and salt and pepper to taste.

Melt the butter in a large non-stick frying pan over medium heat. Pour the egg mixture in and tilt your pan so that the egg flows into the open spaces. It will only take 1–2 minutes to cook. When it is almost done to your liking, add the cheese (if using) and fold it over.

Taste your gravy, adjust the seasoning and add salt and pepper to taste. When you are happy with the consistency of the sauce, pour some of it onto a heated plate and top with the omelette. Drizzle a little more gravy over the top to serve and garnish with the coriander, mint and garam masala.

DOSAS, IDLIS AND MORE

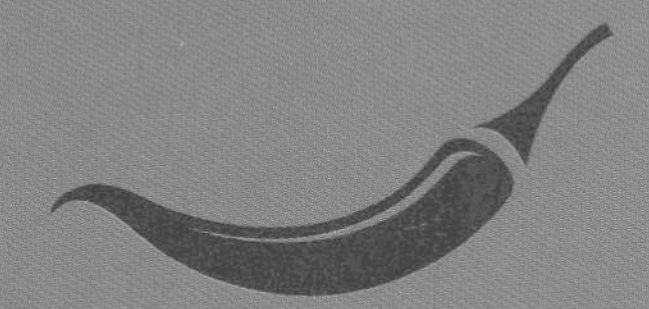

If you've ever tried dosas or idlis at a restaurant, chances are they used instant batters. The best places make their own. I prefer homemade batters as I find them easier to work and more flavourful. Opposite I have given my 'go to' recipe for dosa batter, which also works really well for idlis. Make this batter and I promise you will be in food heaven. If you just want to practise or save yourself a bit of work and time, pick up some instant dosa and/or idli batter. Shop-bought idli batter works really well. I find shop-bought dosa batter difficult to work at times but it does work with a little practice. When using shop-bought dosa batter, follow the cooking instructions on the package. When you make your own batter, you are free to spread and cook the batter in a more authentic way, as per the instructions in this book.

DOSAS
(RICE AND LENTIL CRISPY PANCAKES)

MAKES ENOUGH TO SERVE 10–12 PEOPLE

Dosa batter takes time to make correctly. I have taught many people to make dosas. The difficulty of this job depends on the pans used. As a beginner, I recommend using a large non-stick crêpe pan. Normal high-sided, non-stick pans are more difficult as the sides get in the way of swirling the batter outwards. If that's all you have, make your dosas smaller. I want to make this as easy for you to learn as possible so I have videoed myself making dosas, which you can watch on my YouTube channel. If you really get into making dosas, I recommend picking up a crêpe machine. I couldn't be without mine! The large surface of the crêpe machine makes it possible for you to make large and quite impressive dosas.

There are instant batters available that work really well. You won't get the same sour flavour that you get from the homemade batter but you will still achieve really good dosas with it. Instant batter is great for practising. This recipe is for a large batch. It freezes really well but you might like to use the extra batter to practise your dosa-making skills. Don't worry if they don't look perfect at first – they'll still taste amazing.

PREP TIME: 25 MINS, PLUS 36 HOURS SOAKING AND FERMENTING TIME
COOKING TIME: 5–8 MINS PER DOSA

600g (3½ cups) broken Basmati rice
150g (¾ cup) white split urad dhal lentils
1 heaped tsp fenugreek (methi) seeds
2 tsp sugar
Oil, for cooking and greasing
½ onion, for greasing
2 tsp sea salt

Combine the broken rice, lentils and fenugreek (methi) seeds in a large bowl and rinse three times with water. Pour enough water into the bowl to cover and leave to soak for 12 hours or overnight. Watch it as you might need to add more water as these ingredients soak.

When ready to make your batter, drain the water completely. Fill a jug with 635ml (2½ cups) water. Put about a quarter of the soaked rice and lentil mix into a food processor with about 150ml (⅔ cup) of the water and blend for at least 5 minutes, until very smooth. You do not want to rush this. It is an essential part of making the batter.

Transfer the blended batter to a large bowl and repeat with the rest of the rice and lentil mixture until it is all blended into a batter. Do not use more than the 650ml (2⅔ cups) of water. If you are running low on water at the end and need more liquid to blend, add some of the prepared batter.

Whisk the sugar into your batter and cover with cling film (plastic wrap). The sugar will help the batter ferment as it should. It's best to cover the cling film with a towel and place it outside on a warm day. If the weather is not cooperating, place the batter in a warm cupboard or shelf to ferment for 24 hours. After 24 hours, the batter should be foamy on the top. Whisk in the salt.

Your batter can be kept in an air-tight container in the fridge for up to 3 days and it also freezes well. If not using immediately, you will need to whisk it into a smooth batter again before using.

Recipe continued overleaf

To make the dosas, heat your dosa pan over medium–high heat until a few drops of water evaporate immediately when splashed into the pan. If using a temperature-controlled crêpe maker, set the heat to 180°C (350°F). When your pan is hot, cool it down slightly by wiping the surface with a wet towel and then pour about ¼ teaspoon oil into the pan and rub it all over the surface with the half onion.

The amount of batter you use for each dosa depends on the size of your cooking surface, but for a standard 30-cm (12-in) crêpe pan, use about 200ml (generous ¾ cup). Pour the dosa batter into the pan and spread it outwards from the centre with a flat-bottomed cup or ladle. Don't panic if you are new to this, just do your best to spread the batter out evenly, as thinly as possible, over the surface of the pan. Remember, if you mess up, it will still taste good. The thinner you spread the batter, the crispier the dosa will be.

As the underside cooks, the edges of the dosa will begin to get crispy and break away from the pan. When this happens, trickle about ½ tablespoon of oil around the edges of the dosa.

When the dosa is nicely browned on the underside add any fillings you may be using and distribute evenly over the surface. Just butter is nice but I have given recipes or popular fillings in this book. The filling will quickly heat through. To finish, roll it up or fold it in half to serve.

Keep warm and repeat until all of the batter is used.

NOTE

If the batter clumps when you make your dosas, the heat is too high. Go ahead and cook the dosa. It won't look like much but it will still taste good. Perfect dosas come with practice.

NEER DOSAS
(LIGHT RICE PANCAKES)

MAKES 4–6

Neer dosas take some time to get right. A lot depends on your pan, so I do advise you to use a good non-stick pan with a lid. The more you make them, the better you'll get. The good news is, you really can't go that wrong. Even if they don't look perfect, if you follow these instructions, they'll still taste the same. These dosas are an excellent alternative to white rice – that's essentially what they are after all. Dip them in your curries or just eat them like bread with a little butter. While you're practising, I recommend soaking a few cups of rice rather than just the one. Depending on your hob and pan, you might find you need a little less or more water. Have fun experimenting. You can always snack on those that don't turn out perfectly.

PREP TIME: 5 MINS, PLUS SOAKING TIME
COOKING TIME: 10 MINS

185g (1 cup) Basmati rice, rinsed several times and then soaked overnight
½ tsp salt

Sieve your rice, then blitz it in a blender or spice grinder until you have a smooth paste. Mix this paste with 200ml (generous ¾ cup) water and the salt. It should be about the same consistency as milk. If it is too thin, the dosas will stick to the pan.

Heat a non-stick frying pan over medium–high heat. When hot, take a ladle of the batter and pour it into the pan, starting with the edges and then moving the ladle into the centre. Tilt your pan to fill any empty spaces. You want the dosas to be as thin as possible, so only use enough batter to thinly cover the surface of the pan. Cover the pan and count to 30. That's all the time it takes, as long as your batter is thin enough. Lift the lid. If it still looks raw on top, cover it and cook a little longer. These are bright white dosas so try not to brown them. If you do, oh well!

Using a spatula, carefully fold the dosa in half into a semi-circle. Then fold it over again to make a neat little triangle and transfer to a plate. Repeat to use all the remaining batter.

BEETROOT AND POTATO MASALA DOSAS

SERVES 4–6

I'm a big fan of masala dosas, which are usually served with a nice potato filling. Here beetroot is added. This not only gives the filling an eye-catching colour but tastes fantastic. Dosas are delicious served with a selection of raitas, pickles and chutneys. If it sounds good, make it! In the photo, the dosa is served with coconut and chilli sambol (page 125) and mint raita (page 124). You can also never go wrong serving them with hot sambar (page 80)!

PREP TIME: 10 MINS, PLUS MAKING THE BATTER
COOKING TIME: 20 MINS FOR THE MASALA, AND 5–8 MINS PER DOSA

½ batch of dosa batter (see pages 83–4)
Oil, for cooking and greasing
½ onion, for greasing

FOR THE MASALA
2 tbsp ghee or rapeseed (canola) oil
1 tsp mustard seeds
10 fresh curry leaves
1 tsp cumin seeds
1 onion, finely chopped
2 green chillies, finely chopped
4 large potatoes, peeled and cut into small cubes
2 beetroots (beets), peeled and cut into small cubes
½ tsp ground turmeric
½ tsp chilli powder
3 tbsp chopped fresh coriander (cilantro)
Salt and freshly ground black pepper

To make the masala, heat the ghee or oil in a large wok or frying pan over medium–high heat. When hot, add the mustard seeds. When the seeds begin to pop, stir in the curry leaves and cumin seeds. Fry these for about 40 seconds so that the oil picks up their delicious flavour.

Add the chopped onion and chillies and fry for a further 5 minutes, until the onion is soft and translucent. Add the cubed potatoes and beetroot (beets) along with the turmeric and chilli powder and fry for a few minutes. Now add just enough water to cover and simmer this mixture until the potatoes and beetroot are cooked through and the water has evaporated. This should take about 10 minutes but don't rush things! Your masala is ready when the potato and beetroot is good and soft. Mash lightly, then sprinkle in the fresh coriander (cilantro) and salt and pepper to taste.

Now make the dosas, following the method on pages 83–4. When the dosa is nicely browned on the underside, add the potato masala evenly over the surface. It will quickly heat through. To finish, roll it up or fold it in half to serve. Keep warm and repeat until all of the batter and filling is used.

<30

RAVA DOSAS (CRISPY DOSAS MADE WITH RICE, SEMOLINA, WHEAT AND CHICKPEA FLOURS)

SERVES 4 OR MORE AS PART OF A MULTI-COURSE MEAL

Rava dosas are usually made for breakfast in India but here in the UK they are a popular option on dinner menus. These are super easy to make. You could use any non-stick pan but I prefer to make them with a tawa. Tawas have slightly raised edges and the batter tends to run into the middle, giving you a fluffy, porous centre and really crispy edges. Unlike other dosas, there is no fancy spreading required. The batter needs to be pourable, like a thin tomato soup, and you simply splatter it around your pan and let the dosa cook.

PREP TIME: 5 MINS
COOKING TIME: 10–15 MINS

85g (⅔ cup) rice flour
85g (⅔ cup) fine semolina flour
30g (¼ cup) plain (all-purpose) flour
3 tbsp gram (chickpea) flour
1 tsp cumin seeds
½ tsp salt
2 tbsp finely chopped coriander (cilantro)
2 green bird's-eye chillies, finely chopped
2 tsp finely chopped ginger
½ tsp asafoetida (optional)
5 curry leaves, finely chopped
1 red onion, finely chopped
1 tbsp plain yoghurt
Rapeseed (canola) oil, for frying
½ onion, for greasing (optional)

Thoroughly mix the flours, cumin, salt, coriander (cilantro), chillies, ginger, asafoetida, curry leaves, onion and yoghurt in a large bowl. Add about 200ml (generous ¾ cup) water slowly until you have a very thin batter. It should be just slightly thicker than water.

Heat a tawa or non-stick pan over medium–high heat. Spread about ½ teaspoon oil over the surface. For additional flavour, you can spread the oil using half on onion.

Use a large spoon or ladle to add the batter. Pour a little batter around the edges of the pan and then work your way inward until the surface is covered with a thin layer of batter. Fry until the underside is nicely browned and then flip it over to cook the other side for about 30 seconds. Flip over again and fold in half or into triangles, as shown opposite. Keep warm while you make the remaining dosas.

NOTE

As the batter sits, it will become thicker as the flours absorb the water, so whisk and add more water if necessary before making each dosa. The batter will keep in the fridge for 3 days but be sure to whisk and add more water when needed before making each dosa.

MAKE IT VEGAN

Use vegan yoghurt in place of the plain yoghurt.

SZECHUAN DOSAS

SERVES 4–6

Indo–Chinese fusion food is hugely popular in India. As with all good things, these fusion dishes eventually make their way to the UK. If you enjoy Szechuan food and dosas, this will be the perfect dish for you. I also like to mix the Szechuan paste into white rice.

PREP TIME: 10 MINS, PLUS MAKING THE BATTER AND SOAKING THE CHILLIES
COOKING TIME: 5 MINS FOR THE SZECHUAN PASTE, AND 5–8 MINS PER DOSA

- ½ batch of dosa batter (see pages 83–4)
- Oil, for cooking and greasing
- ½ onion, for greasing

FOR THE SZECHUAN PASTE

- 50g (1¾oz) dried red chillies (medium spicy), about 30
- 12 fat garlic cloves, finely chopped
- 7.5cm (3in) piece of ginger, finely chopped
- 2 tbsp rapeseed (canola) oil
- 3 tbsp tomato ketchup
- 1 tbsp dark soy sauce
- 1 tbsp rice, coconut or white wine vinegar
- Salt

To make the Szechuan paste, soak the dried chillies in water for 30 minutes. Then blend them with just enough of the soaking water to form a thick paste.

In a large frying pan, sauté the garlic and ginger in the oil over medium heat for about 1 minute, until soft and fragrant. Stir in the chilli paste and fry for a further minute before adding the ketchup, soy sauce and vinegar. Check for seasoning and add salt to taste.

Now make the dosas, following the method on pages 83–4. When the dosa is nicely browned on the underside, spread a few tablespoons of the Szechuan paste evenly over the surface. It will quickly heat through. To finish, roll it up or fold it in half to serve. Keep warm and repeat until all of the batter and filling is used.

GUNPOWDER AND GHEE FRIED TATTE IDLIS

(CRISPY FRIED RICE AND LENTIL CAKES WITH SPICY ROASTED LENTIL GARNISH)

SERVES 4–8

Steamed tatte idlis are normally quite large, floppy and fluffy. They are about five times larger than the Kanchipuram idlis on page 94 and a special large idli mould is needed to make them. You could use normal-sized idlis for this recipe if you wish though. I made loads of idlis during the photoshoot for this book and, for a bit of snacking fun, I decided to cut some up and fry them for the team and whoa...! It was agreed that this technique needed to be included here. The frying gives the idlis a delicious crispy exterior while retaining the fluffy centre. It's my favourite way to serve them. Simply steamed or fried, this recipe, together with the gunpowder is one I return to again and again. The idlis are also delicious with sambar (see page 80) and a selection of chutneys. I've used my homemade dosa batter for this recipe but if you wish you could use instant idli batter to make things even easier.

PREP TIME: 20 MINS
COOKING TIME: 10–15 MINS

Rapeseed (canola) oil, for greasing the idli moulds and for frying
½ batch dosa batter (see pages 83–4)
Melted ghee or vegetable ghee, to serve

FOR THE GUNPOWDER SPICE BLEND
75g (heaped ½ cup) sesame seeds
100g (½ cup) white split urad dhal lentils
100g (½ cup) chana dhal
1 large handful of dried Kashmiri chillies (more or less to taste)
30 curry leaves
Salt

For the gunpowder spice blend, toast the sesame seeds, urad dhal and chana dhal separately in a dry frying pan until they are toasty brown and fragrant. The sesame seeds and urad dhal will brown in about 30–60 seconds and the chana dhal needs longer – around 1½–2 minutes. Transfer to a bowl to cool.

Toast the Kashmiri chillies in the same way for about a minute and leave to cool with the other ingredients. Toast the curry leaves, also for a minute, until almost dried but still fresh-looking.

When cool, place everything in a spice grinder and grind to a powder. Season with salt to taste. This will keep for at least 2 months in an air-tight container.

When ready to cook, oil your idli moulds lightly so that the idli don't stick when cooking. Pour a little water into a large pan so that the water comes up almost to the top of your bottom mould. Bring the water to the boil. Pour the batter carefully into the moulds, place into the steaming pan and cover. Let steam for about 10 minutes. The idlis will puff up, as photographed. To check that they are done, stick a toothpick or fork into an idli. If it comes out clean, they are ready. If you pull it out and there is a little idli batter stuck to it, cook for another minute or so. Be careful not to overcook the idlis as they will become dry. Allow them to sit in the moulds for a couple of minutes after cooking and then carefully remove the idlis from the moulds.

For a lighter and much more traditional way of serving these idlis, your job is done. Simply top with melted ghee and a good dose of gunpowder to serve. For a more crispy exterior, I like to shallow-fry the idlis in about 2.5cm (1in) of rapeseed (canola) oil before topping with ghee and gunpowder, as shown.

KANCHIPURAM IDLIS

(FLUFFY RICE AND LENTIL CAKES WITH CASHEWS, CORIANDER, CHILLIES AND SPICES)

SERVES 4 OR MORE AS PART OF A MULTI-COURSE MEAL

Normal fluffy white idlis are great. This recipe takes the simple idli to a whole new level. I often make both plain and Kanchipuram idlis when I'm having friends around. The difference in flavour is quite substantial and these special idlis are also quite colourful, which is nice when you're laying out a big curry spread.

PREP TIME: 10 MINS, PLUS MAKING THE BATTER
COOKING TIME: 20 MINS

2 tbsp rapeseed (canola) oil
1 tsp chana dhal
1 tsp white split urad dhal lentils
1 tsp cumin seeds
2 green chillies, finely chopped
3 tbsp cashews, lightly crushed
10 curry leaves
3 tbsp chopped fresh coriander (cilantro)
1 tsp ground turmeric
½ tsp ground ginger
½ batch dosa batter (see pages 83–4), or instant idli batter (about 700ml/scant 3 cups)
Sambar (see page 80), to serve
A selection of pickles and chutneys, to serve

Heat 1 tablespoon of the oil in a large frying pan. Add the chana dhal and fry for about a minute, then add the urad dhal. Continue frying, moving the lentils around in the pan for another minute. The lentils will begin to turn a light brown and become fragrant. Now add the cumin seeds, green chillies and crushed cashews and fry for a further 30 seconds before adding the curry leaves and chopped coriander (cilantro). Give it all a good stir over the heat, then take off the heat and allow to cool slightly.

Whisk the ground turmeric and ginger into the dosa or idli batter and then add the fried lentil mixture.

Using the remaining oil, lightly grease your idli moulds. You only need a film of oil in each reservoir – no oil puddles!

Bring enough water to a boil so that it is just under where your lowest idli tray will sit. Pour the batter into the moulds and carefully lower into a steamer to steam for 10 minutes. After 10 minutes, stick a toothpick or fork into a couple of the idlis. If it comes out clean, your idlis are ready. If there is a film of batter on it, cover and steam the idlis for a couple more minutes, until your toothpick/fork comes out clean.

Remove the idli tray from the steamer and allow to rest for a couple of minutes before attempting to remove them. This will make it easier to get them out of the recesses. Carefully remove the idlis from the tray with a knife or small spoon.

Serve the idlis with sambar and a selection of pickles and/or chutneys.

EGG HOPPERS
(BREAKFAST PANCAKE WITH EGG AND COCONUT)

MAKES ABOUT 8 HOPPERS

I first tried egg hoppers in Sri Lanka and now make them regularly. A special small wok with a rounded bottom and a lid is used there so I made sure to bring some back. I haven't seen any of these in shops in the UK but you can purchase them online. Do try to find a hopper pan if you can, but if not, give this a try regardless: you may not get the eye-catching authentic bowl-shaped hopper but it will still cook nicely in any pan and the flavour will be the same. A small flat-bottomed wok with a lid will work well. I've seen chefs make flat hoppers and they were still delicious. Serve these with your favourite chutney or raita. In my opinion, the coconut and chilli sambol on page 125 is a must.

PREP TIME: 10 MINS, PLUS RISING TIME
COOKING TIME: 35 MINS

500g (3¾ cups) fine rice flour
800ml (3½ cups) tinned (canned) coconut milk
1 tsp dried yeast
A pinch of sugar
Vegetable oil, for frying
8 eggs
Salt and freshly ground black pepper
Chutney or raita, to serve (optional)

Sift the flour into a large bowl.

Heat the coconut milk in a pan over low heat until hand-hot, then sprinkle the yeast into it. Mix until the yeast dissolves, then pour it into the flour. Add the sugar and whisk to a smooth batter without any lumps. Cover and leave in a warm location to rise. I find placing it in my oven with just the pilot light on is perfect, or you could place it in an electric oven on the lowest heat. The batter can be used in about 8 hours but it is tastier after it bubbles and ferments for 24 hours.

After the batter has bubbled up nicely, whisk it again until you have a batter that is the consistency of single (light) cream. Be sure to whisk out any lumps. If the batter is too thick, add a little water to achieve a creamy consistency.

When you are ready to cook, heat your wok/hopper pan over medium–high heat and just add a drop of oil. You only need to coat the wok so I usually wipe the oil around with a paper towel. Pour in a ladle full of the batter and swirl it around the wok until the sides are nicely coated with a thin layer of the batter. If you are using a hopper pan, try to get the batter to coat the whole inside of the pan. Break an egg into a bowl and tip it into the batter at the bottom, then cover the wok/pan. Allow to cook for about 4 minutes, covered. You can check it occasionally but the lid needs to be on for most of the cooking time. The hopper is ready when the sides begin to peel away from the wok/sides. If you are not using a non-stick wok/pan, you may need to tap the sides a few times to help release the hopper. Carefully carve around the sides until it is free from the wok.

Re-oil the wok and repeat to cook the remaining hoppers – you should be able to make about 8 from the batter.

Season with salt and pepper to taste and serve with your favourite chutney or raita.

MAKE IT VEGAN

Many people love these without the egg. Just fry the batter and enjoy!

OUTDOOR COOKING

Each of the recipes in this section is perfect for outdoor cooking and dining. You only need to know the basics of barbecue cooking to get them just right. Here I would like to give you that information. These recipes can also be made in an oven and I have included instructions on doing that, just in case cooking outdoors isn't your thing.

PREPARING YOUR BARBECUE FOR DIRECT HEAT GRILLING

This is the way most of us cook on the barbecue. Cooking over hot coals will get you that nice char that looks great and tastes fantastic. You might be interested to learn that many of the dishes that are called 'tandoori' in restaurants are actually just marinated in a tandoori-style marinade and then grilled over hot coals.

When I barbecue in this way, I use a lot of charcoal – about two shoeboxes full – as it is vital to achieve an intense heat. Light your mound of charcoal and let it heat up until your coals are white-hot. When visibly hot, spread the charcoal out evenly under the grill with a pair of tongs or something similar. If you hold your hand about 5cm (2in) above the fire and it is unbearably hot after 2 seconds, you're ready to cook.

PREPARING YOUR BARBECUE FOR INDIRECT COOKING

This is the method to use for roasting. You will need a barbecue with a tight-fitting lid. Fill your barbecue basin with about two shoeboxes full of charcoal on one side, leaving the other side empty. Light the charcoal and let it heat up until white-hot, then place the barbecue grill over the top. Place whatever it is you are roasting on the side with no coals and cover. If you are barbecuing in this way over an extended period of time, you will need to add a few handfuls of charcoal every half hour or so.

PREPARING YOUR HOME TANDOOR OVEN FOR COOKING

Open the bottom vent completely and place a few fire starters in the tandoor opposite the vent. Pour in about two shoeboxes full of charcoal and light, ensuring that you strategically stack as many pieces of charcoal as you can over the flames. It is important that your charcoal is as far away from the vent as possible so that air can flow freely.

Once the fire is burning nicely, place the lid on, leaving a crack open so that air can flow from the vent to the top. Close the bottom vent so that it is only one-third open. It will need an hour or more to get up to heat. To work properly, the clay walls of the oven need to be extremely hot and the tandoor needs to be at least 230°C (450°F) for cooking vegetables and even hotter for naans.

If you are cooking with a tandoor for the first time, be sure to read the manual first. You will need to cure the clay walls before cooking anything.

OVEN COOKING

Ovens vary but I usually crank mine up to 200°C (400°F/Gas 6) and cook on a wire rack near the top. To get that charred appearance and flavour, place the vegetables under a hot grill (broiler) for a couple of minutes after cooking, just before serving.

SPECIAL INSTRUCTIONS ON COOKING NAAN PIZZA

In the naan pizza recipes on pages 112–15, I give instructions for the way I find it easiest to cook them. The bases are pre-cooked indoors on the hob, like stovetop naans, and then finished outdoors on the barbecue. Pizzas need a lot of heat to cook to perfection, which can be difficult to do on a kettle barbecue. If you want to cook the pizzas completely outdoors, set up your barbecue for indirect cooking (see above left). Place the rolled pizza bases over the hot part for about 2 minutes, then flip them over and cook for another minute. Then follow the recipe.

MUSTARD AND GARLIC ROAST BROCCOLI

SERVES 4

As recipes go, this is an easy one. I learned to make it with cauliflower, which is used a lot more in India, so this can be substituted if you wish. I prefer to use broccoli; the flavour of the smoky, charred broccoli adds so much to this dish. You could make this a saucy dish by doubling or tripling the marinade recipe. Then slowly heat it up in a pan after it's done its job marinating and pour it over the cooked broccoli. This broccoli is delicious served with curry mayonnaise (see page 108) or with mixed vegetable sabzi (see page 64).

PREP TIME: 5 MINS, PLUS MARINATING TIME
COOKING TIME: 20 MINS

Salt
2 large heads of broccoli
Flaky sea salt

FOR THE MARINADE
125g (½ cup) Greek yoghurt
1 tbsp wholegrain mustard
½ tsp ground turmeric
1 tsp ground cumin
1 tsp ground coriander
½ tsp chaat masala
1 tsp chilli powder
2 tbsp finely grated Parmesan cheese (optional)
1½ tbsp minced garlic or garlic paste
1 tsp dried fenugreek leaves (kasoori methi)
1½ tbsp mustard oil or rapeseed (canola) oil

Bring a large saucepan of lightly salted water to a boil. Cut each head of broccoli into steaks (as in the picture on page 102) and blanch in the water for 3 minutes. Remove and set aside to cool slightly.

Whisk all of the marinade ingredients together in a large bowl and add the broccoli. Mix it well and allow to marinate for about 20 minutes, until browned. If working ahead of time, you can marinate it for longer.

Light about a shoebox full of charcoal in your barbecue. When the coals are white-hot, put the broccoli steaks on the grill for about 10–15 minutes, turning regularly to get an even char. You could also place the broccoli in an oven preheated to 200°C (400°F/Gas 6) for about 20 minutes, until browned. To finish, season with flaky sea salt to taste.

MAKE IT VEGAN

You could use dairy-free yoghurt and omit the Parmesan. That said, I have tried a good dairy-free Parmesan, although it was quite salty.

GF

TANDOORI MUSHROOMS WITH PAPRIKA SAUCE

SERVES 4 OR MORE AS PART OF A MULTI-COURSE MEAL

This is such a simple recipe but the ingredients work so well together. Whenever I make these mushrooms for friends, they all go – and very quickly too!

PREP TIME: 5 MINS, PLUS MARINATING TIME
COOKING TIME: 8 MINS

250g (9oz) chestnut (cremini) mushrooms, or similar

FOR THE MARINADE
2 tbsp garlic and ginger paste
1 green chilli, finely chopped
1 tsp ground cumin
1 tbsp smoked sweet paprika
½ tsp amchoor (dried mango powder) or citric acid
1 tsp garam masala
Juice of 3 limes
1 tsp mustard oil
200ml (generous ¾ cup) plain Greek yoghurt
3 tbsp finely chopped coriander (cilantro)
Salt and freshly ground black pepper

Set up your barbecue for the direct cooking method (see page 99) or preheat your oven to its highest setting.

In a large bowl, combine all of the marinade ingredients and whisk to combine.

Now place your mushrooms in the marinade. Allow to marinate for about an hour, stirring to coat from time to time.

Skewer the mushrooms onto metal skewers and place over the hot coals. If using your oven, thread the mushrooms onto soaked wooden skewers and place on a rack at the top of your oven.

Spoon the remaining marinade into a small saucepan and heat until hot but not boiling. Set aside while the mushrooms cook.

After about 8 minutes, the mushrooms should be ready. Season with salt and pepper to taste and serve with the warmed marinade.

MAKE IT VEGAN
Use dairy-free yoghurt in place of the Greek yoghurt.

PANEER HARIYALI

(PANEER AND VEGETABLES MARINATED IN A SPICY MINT AND CORIANDER DRESSING)

SERVES 4 OR MORE AS PART OF A MULTI-COURSE MEAL

The mint and coriander sauce on page 9 isn't just delicious served as a sauce. It makes an amazing marinade as well. Paneer hariyali usually has a stronger flavour of coriander (cilantro) than mint, so I suggest using a 70% to 30% coriander to mint ratio when preparing your sauce. Then all you need to do is add a few more ingredients, marinate the paneer and vegetables for 30 minutes or more and you're ready to cook one of my favourite barbecued paneer dishes! This one is best cooked over high heat on skewers but could also be pan fried in a little oil.

PREP TIME: 10 MINS, PLUS MARINATING TIME
COOKING TIME: 10–12 MINS

- 400g (14oz) paneer, cut into small cubes
- 1 red onion, quartered and cut into pieces the size of the paneer
- 1 green (bell) pepper, cut into small pieces the size of the paneer
- 8 cherry tomatoes
- Salt
- Naans or chapattis, to serve (optional)

FOR THE MARINADE

- 250ml (1 cup) mint and coriander sauce (1 recipe quantity on page 9 and see intro above)
- ½ tsp amchoor (dried mango powder)
- 1 tbsp ground cumin
- 1 tsp chaat masala
- ¼ tsp ajwain (carom) seeds
- 1 tsp dried fenugreek leaves (kasoori methi)
- 2 tbsp gram (chickpea) flour
- 1 tbsp vegetable oil

Set your barbecue up for direct heat cooking (see page 99).

Whisk all of the marinade ingredients together in a large bowl and add the paneer, red onion, (bell) pepper and tomatoes. Ensure the cheese and veggies are completely coated with the marinade. This can all be done a few hours ahead of cooking but you can get away with about 10 minutes of marinating.

Skewer the paneer, onion, (bell) pepper and tomato. When ready to cook, place the skewers over the hot coals and cook for about 10 minutes, turning regularly until the paneer cubes are cooked through, soft and nicely charred.

Season with salt to taste and eat the kebabs on their own or wrap into homemade naans or chapattis.

GRILLED SPICE AND LIME CORN ON THE COB

SERVES 4–6 AS PART OF A MULTI-COURSE MEAL

When you try this corn on the cob, you'll never go back! In barbecue season, I like to light up a lumpwood or log fire and cook the corn directly on the hot coals. Don't worry about burning the corn. You want about a quarter of the kernels to blacken as it cooks through. Only cook on the coals if you are using untreated charcoal.

PREP TIME: 5 MINS
COOKING TIME: 10 MINS

75g (5 tbsp) unsalted butter
4 long corn on the cobs (ears of corn)
2 limes, quartered

FOR THE SPICE MIX
1 tsp amchoor (dried mango powder)
1 tsp ground cumin
½ tsp chaat masala
1 tsp chilli powder
1 tsp salt

Set up your barbecue for direct cooking (see page 99). Place a tray near the fire with the butter on and let it melt.

Mix together all the spice mix ingredients on a serving plate and set aside.

When ready to cook, place your corn either on the grate or right in the coals. As you hear the corn begin to crackle, turn it slightly and continue doing this until you have a mixture of yellow and blackened corn kernels.

To serve, roll the corn around in the melted butter. Serve hot and tell friends to dip their corn in the spice mixture and then rub it all over the corn with the lime wedges, squeezing the juice out as they do.

MAKE IT VEGAN

Although the butter could be simply omitted, this corn should taste buttery to be authentic. If you'd like, you could try a non-dairy butter or vegetable ghee.

GF

GRILLED MUSHROOMS WITH FIG AND MOZZARELLA STUFFING AND CURRY-LEAF DRESSING

SERVES 2–4

I have to say that this is one of my all-time favourite mushroom recipes. I first tried it at a local curry house that's no longer around but I did get to watch the chef there make this. I later heard that a similar dish was being served at a tandoori restaurant in Camden called Namaaste Kitchen. Knowing the brilliant restaurant and its talented chef/owner, Sabbir Karim, my bet is that the dish originated there. I didn't get Sabbir's recipe in time for this cookbook but I think you are going to like this one.

PREP TIME: 15 MINS
COOKING TIME: 20 MINS

4 large flat mushrooms, with the stems cut off and chopped for the stuffing
150g (5½oz) fresh buffalo mozzarella, roughly chopped
3 spring onions (scallions), roughly chopped
3 soft dried figs, finely chopped
1 green chilli, finely chopped
Salt

FOR THE MARINADE
1 tbsp olive oil
1½ tbsp garlic and ginger paste
A pinch of ground cumin
A pinch of garam masala

FOR THE DRESSING
1 large bunch of fresh curry leaves (about 50)
1 garlic clove, smashed
1cm (½in) piece of ginger, grated
2 tbsp extra virgin olive oil
2 tbsp lime juice
A pinch of salt
A pinch of red chilli powder
½ tsp ground cumin
Salt and freshly ground black pepper, to taste

Set up your barbecue for indirect cooking (see page 99).

While it is heating up, mix all of the marinade ingredients in a bowl, then add the mushroom tops. Coat them evenly and allow the mushrooms to marinate while you make the filling.

Mix the mozzarella, spring onions (scallions), figs, chopped mushroom stems and green chilli together in a bowl and season with salt to taste. Now remove the mushroom tops from the marinade and fill them equally with the stuffing.

When your barbecue is up to heat, place the stuffed mushrooms over the cooler side and bake for about 20 minutes, until cooked through and browned on the top.

While the mushrooms are baking, make the dressing. This can also be done a day or so in advance. Place the curry leaves in a pestle and mortar and pound until the leaves are broken into small pieces, but not a paste. This helps release their flavour. Now add the garlic and ginger and pound some more to incorporate. Add the rest of the ingredients and whisk them all together until you have a nice thick, leafy dressing. Check for seasoning and set aside until ready to use.

Place each of the baked mushrooms on a plate and drizzle the curry-leaf dressing over them to serve.

NOTE

You can also make this recipe in the oven. Place a baking tray with a wire rack in the oven and pre-heat it to 200°C (400°F/Gas 6). When your oven is up to heat, place the stuffed mushrooms on the rack over the baking tray and bake for about 20 minutes, until cooked through and toasty brown on top.

MAKE IT VEGAN

The mozzarella could simply be left out or there is good dairy-free mozzarella available that melts well and makes a great alternative.

GRILLED ARTICHOKES WITH CURRY MAYONNAISE

SERVES 4–6

Where I grew up in California, globe artichokes were really easy to come by. Here in the UK, I've only seen them in London and on the rare occasion in a supermarket closer to home. You can order them online too. So nowadays, globe artichokes are for special occasions. If you happen to have a special gathering planned, you've got to serve this one!

PREP TIME: 10 MINS, PLUS MARINATING TIME
COOKING TIME: 35 MINS

4 large globe artichokes
3 tbsp finely chopped coriander (cilantro)

FOR THE MARINADE
2 tbsp lemon juice
125ml (½ cup) extra virgin olive oil
6 garlic cloves, finely chopped
1 tsp salt
1 tsp freshly ground black pepper

FOR THE CURRY MAYONNAISE
250ml (1 cup) mayonnaise
1 tsp curry powder
½ tsp chilli powder
1 green chilli, finely chopped
1–2 tsp lime juice

Cut off the thick outer leaves of the artichokes and cut off all but a little of the stems if the stems are long, as shown. This part of the stem is just an extension of the delicious heart. If it looks like the skin on the stem is tough, you can peel them. Bring a large pan of water to the boil and cook the artichokes for 20 minutes, or until the outer leaves peel off easily. Allow to cool slightly so that the artichokes are easier to handle, then cut them in half. Cut out any of the hair-like bits from the centre. That is the 'choke' from artichoke, so discard it.

Whisk together all the marinade ingredients and and rub all over the artichoke halves. Let this marinate for about 30 minutes.

Meanwhile, mix all of the the curry mayonnaise ingredients together and place, covered, in the fridge until ready to serve.

Light up about a shoebox full of charcoal in your barbecue. When the coals are white-hot, place the artichokes, cut-side down, on the grill. Be sure to retain any leftover marinade. Cook over the hot coals for about 15 minutes, turning often, until they are nicely charred. With artichokes, they really are done when they're done, so continue cooking until the base (the heart) is fork tender.

To serve, spoon a little of the leftover marinade over the artichokes and serve with the curried mayonnaise. Garnish with the chopped coriander (cilantro).

Just in case you've never tried globe artichokes before, peel off each leaf, dip it in some of the mayonnaise and scrape off the flesh with your teeth. You can discard the remaining leaf. When all of the leaves have been devoured, cut up the artichoke heart and serve it with more of the mayonnaise.

MAKE IT VEGAN
Use the spicy cashew dip on page 125 instead of the mayonnaise, or there are vegan mayonnaises on the market.

HASSELBACK BUTTERNUT SQUASH

SERVES 2–4

This is a nice one for the barbecue; the smoky flavour you get complements this dish superbly! I often use the same ingredients but cut the squash into cubes instead. It's less of a faff, but I think you'll agree hasselback slicing the squash turns a pretty basic dish into an eye-catching centrepiece. Using a sharp knife will make slicing easier and much more uniform. Placing a wooden spoon at the base of the squash will help ensure you don't cut too deep. If you do accidently cut the squash in half, all is not ruined! Just place the pieces together so it looks whole again.

PREP TIME: 15 MINS
COOKING TIME: 1 HOUR

- 1 large butternut squash (about 800g/1lb 12oz)
- 2 tbsp rapeseed (canola) oil
- 1 tsp brown mustard seeds
- 1 tbsp cumin seeds
- 20 fresh or frozen curry leaves
- 2 tbsp garlic and ginger paste
- 2 green chillies, finely chopped
- 1 tsp chilli powder
- 2 tbsp butter
- 3 tbsp date molasses or brown sugar
- 15 cashews, lightly crushed
- Salt and freshly ground black pepper
- 3 tbsp finely chopped coriander (cilantro), to serve

Prepare you barbecue for indirect heat cooking (see page 99).

Cut the squash in half lengthwise and remove the seeds from the centre. You could peel the skin but I rarely do. It crisps right up and has a lot of goodness in it. Place the two halves, cut-side down, on a chopping board and, using a very sharp knife, make slits every 7–10mm (½in). Be careful not to cut all the way through.

Heat the oil in a large frying pan over medium–high heat. When visibly hot, add the mustard seeds. When they begin to pop in the hot oil, stir in the cumin seeds and curry leaves and let them sizzle in the oil for about 30 seconds, until fragrant. Add the garlic and ginger paste, chillies and chilli powder and continue cooking for another 30 seconds.

Place the squash, slit-side up, on a baking tray and rub this nicely seasoned oil all over. Try to get the oil deep into the slits. Place the tray in your barbecue and cover. Cook for 40–50 minutes, or until the squash is cooked through and beginning to colour. You might need to add a little charcoal during cooking.

Meanwhile, melt the butter in a saucepan and stir in the molasses or brown sugar and the crushed cashews. When your squash is looking like it's ready, smother it with the butter mixture and cook for a further 5 minutes.

To serve, transfer the squash halves to a warm serving platter. Season with salt and pepper to taste and garnish with the chopped coriander (cilantro).

PANEER, ONION, CHILLI AND GARLIC NAAN PIZZA

MAKES 4 X 25CM (10IN) PIZZAS (SERVES 4–6)

I hesitated before putting recipes for pizzas in my book. They're Italian, aren't they? It wasn't until the last time I went to Mumbai that I realized just how popular Indian fusion pizzas are. I ate my fair share, or perhaps a few more. From India to New York, Indian pizzas are becoming very popular, and now you can have a go at making your own.

PREP TIME: 20 MINS, PLUS PREPARING THE DOUGH
COOKING TIME: 5–10 MINS PER PIZZA

- 1 recipe quantity naan dough (see page 131)
- Plain (all-purpose) flour, for dusting
- 8 garlic cloves, finely chopped
- 1 large red onion, finely chopped
- 4 red chillies, finely chopped (or to taste)
- 250g (9oz) paneer, cut into small cubes
- 2 tbsp extra virgin olive oil
- 4 tbsp freshly grated Parmesan

FOR THE SAUCE

- 3 tbsp extra virgin olive oil
- 2 garlic cloves, smashed
- 3 tbsp finely chopped coriander (cilantro) stalks
- 2 x 400g (14oz) tins (cans) of plum tomatoes, blended, or unseasoned passata
- Salt and freshly ground black pepper

To make the sauce, heat the 3 tablespoons of olive oil in a saucepan over medium–high heat and toss in the smashed garlic cloves. Allow the oil to take on the flavour of the garlic for a couple of minutes and then add the chopped coriander (cilantro) stalks. Fry for a further minute, then pour in the blended tomatoes. Simmer this sauce for about 10 minutes or until the sauce thickens to how you would expect a pizza sauce to be. Season with salt and pepper to taste.

Divide the dough into four balls and let rest, covered, for about 5 minutes. Lightly dust the work surface with flour and then, using a rolling pin or your hands, roll or stretch the dough out thinly until you have four pizza bases about 25cm (10in) in diameter.

I find it a lot easier to pre-cook my pizza bases in a pan, as with my stovetop garlic naans on page 131. Pre-cooking the crusts makes them easier to work with outside. Pizzas need a lot of heat, which is difficult to achieve on most kettle barbecues, so this head start helps give them that delicious-looking char as if they came right out of a pizza oven.

Set up your barbecue for indirect cooking (see page 99). I usually use about 3 shoeboxes full of charcoal as the barbecue needs to be good and hot!

When your barbecue is flaming hot, spread the sauce equally all over the four pizza bases. Top with the finely chopped garlic, red onion, chillies and the paneer. Place one or two of the bases directly on cooler side of the grill and close the top. Cook for about 5 minutes or until the cheese is soft and the crust nicely browned. With barbecue, it's ready when it's ready, so don't be afraid to leave the pizza on longer if it looks like it could use more heat.

Drizzle the top with a little olive oil and sprinkle with the grated Parmesan. Repeat to cook the remaining pizzas and serve hot.

MAKE IT VEGAN

Many people substitute tofu for paneer. This changes the dish but it is still very good. If you prefer a cheesier pizza without the paneer, try vegan mozzarella.

CORIANDER PESTO, CHILLI AND FRESH TOMATO NAAN PIZZA

MAKES 4 X 25CM (10IN) PIZZAS (SERVES 4–6)

I'm a big fan of pesto pizzas and this coriander version is a real crowd-pleaser. You can easily double or triple the recipe. The pizzas cook quite quickly on the barbecue but you're going to be busy. I can only fit one pizza on my kettle barbecue so I cook one, place it on the table and repeat. This easy recipe is great for hot summer weekends. All it needs is some good music and ice-cold beer – or whatever your poison happens to be – and you can fill your day, grazing with friends.

PREP TIME: 10 MINS, PLUS PREPARING THE DOUGH
COOKING TIME: 5 MINS PER PIZZA

1 recipe quantity naan dough (see page 131)
Plain (all-purpose) flour, for dusting
250g (9oz) fresh buffalo mozzarella
2–3 very fresh tomatoes, sliced

FOR THE PESTO
200g (7oz) chopped coriander (cilantro) leaves and stalks
3 garlic cloves
1–2 green chillies
30g (¼ cup) roasted, unsalted cashews
30g (scant ½ cup) grated Parmesan (optional)
125ml (½ cup) extra virgin olive oil
Salt

Set up your barbecue for indirect heat cooking (see page 99). I usually use about 3 shoeboxes full of charcoal. You need to get your barbecue as hot as possible.

Meanwhile, to make the pesto, place the coriander (cilantro), garlic, chillies, cashews, Parmesan and oil in a blender and blend into a pesto. Season with salt to taste and set aside.

Divide the dough into four balls and let rest, covered, for about 5 minutes. Lightly dust the surface with flour and then, using a rolling pin or your hands, roll or stretch the dough out thinly until you have four pizza bases around 25cm (10in) in diameter.

I find it a lot easier to pre-cook my pizza bases in a pan, as with my stovetop garlic naans on page 131. Pre-cooking the crusts makes them easier to work with outside. Pizzas need a lot of heat, which is difficult to achieve on most kettle barbecues, so this head start helps give them that delicious-looking char as if they came right out of a pizza oven.

When your barbecue is flaming hot, spread the pesto equally over the pizza bases and top with the mozzarella and tomato slices. Place one or two of the pizzas on the cooler side of the grill and cover. Cook for about 5 minutes or until the cheese is soft and the crust nicely browned. Repeat to cook the remaining pizzas and serve hot.

MAKE IT VEGAN
You could leave the cheese off but there is good-quality vegan mozzarella on the market that melts well and is very convincing.

ACCOMPANIMENTS AND SIDE DISHES

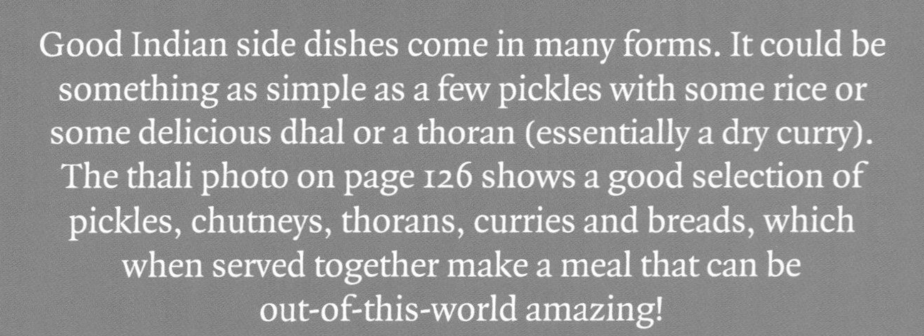

Good Indian side dishes come in many forms. It could be something as simple as a few pickles with some rice or some delicious dhal or a thoran (essentially a dry curry). The thali photo on page 126 shows a good selection of pickles, chutneys, thorans, curries and breads, which when served together make a meal that can be out-of-this-world amazing!

These may be sides but, as you'll see, some can really stand on their own as dishes that are pleasing to the palate. And they're all made with very little fuss.

SPINACH AND SWEETCORN

SERVES 4 OR MORE AS PART OF A MULTI-COURSE MEAL

I use frozen spinach for this dish as it has already been blanched, which is a real timesaver. I usually serve this simple curry as a side dish but it can hold its own as a main.

PREP TIME: 10 MINS
COOKING TIME: 20 MINS

4 large corn on the cobs (ears of corn)
2 tbsp unsalted butter
325g (11½oz) frozen spinach, defrosted
2 tbsp rapeseed (canola) oil
1 tsp cumin seeds
1 onion, finely chopped
2 tbsp garlic and ginger paste
2 green chillies, finely chopped
1 tsp amchoor (dried mango powder)
Juice of 1 lemon or lime
75ml (5 tbsp) double (heavy) cream
1 tsp dried fenugreek leaves (kasoori methi)
Salt

Using a sharp knife, cut the corn from the cobs. Melt the butter over medium–high heat in a frying pan and sauté the corn for about 7 minutes, until it is cooked through. Transfer to a dish and set aside.

Blend the spinach with just enough water to make a smooth paste and set this aside too.

Pour the oil into the pan you used for the corn. When visibly hot, add the cumin seeds. When they begin to crackle, stir in the onion and fry for about 5 minutes, until soft, translucent and lightly browned. Add the garlic and ginger paste, chillies and amchoor (dried mango powder) and cook for a further minute or so.

Pour in the puréed spinach and the corn and stir well to combine. To finish, squeeze in the lemon or lime juice and the cream. Rub the dried fenugreek leaves (kasoori methi) between your fingers and sprinkle over the top. Season with salt to taste.

MAKE IT VEGAN

If you love spinach and corn, you could just leave out the butter and cream. I have had great success using dairy-free butter and vegan cream, both made from oats and soy.

BEETROOT THORAN

(DRY BEETROOT AND COCONUT CURRY)

SERVES 2–4

Bad memories of being served pickled, tinned (canned) beetroot (beet) as a kid made me hesitate before trying my first beetroot thoran. I just couldn't bring myself to order it for many years. Deep down, I knew I had to give it a try as it is so popular at many south Indian restaurants. I'm happy to say that I needn't have been scared to try it! This recipe is so easy and tastes amazing. You can see a photo of this thoran on page 126.

PREP TIME: 5 MINS
COOKING TIME: 10–15 MINS

2 tbsp coconut oil
1 tsp brown mustard seeds
20 fresh or frozen curry leaves
1 red onion, finely chopped
2 green chillies, finely chopped
100g (1 cup) grated fresh or frozen coconut
½ tsp ground turmeric
1 tsp chilli powder
2 large beetroots (beets), peeled and cut into very small 5mm (⅛in) cubes
Salt and freshly ground black pepper
3 tbsp chopped coriander (cilantro), to serve

Heat the coconut oil in a large frying pan over medium–high heat. Add the mustard seeds. When they begin to pop, toss in the curry leaves and let them fry in the oil for about 30 seconds or until fragrant. Add the onion, chillies, grated coconut, turmeric and chilli powder and continue frying for a further 5 minutes, until the onion is soft and translucent.

Add the cubed beetroot (beets) and just enough water to cover. Stir well and cover with a lid. Simmer until the water has almost all evaporated and the beetroot is cooked through.

Season with salt and pepper to taste and serve garnished with the chopped coriander (cilantro).

CABBAGE THORAN
(DRY CABBAGE CURRY WITH SPICES)

SERVES 4 OR MORE AS PART OF A MULTI-COURSE MEAL

I learned this simple but absolutely delicious curry at a brilliant restaurant called Ury in Newcastle. The chef offered to let me watch him make a few dishes and I wasn't going to turn down that offer! I love the place. I like to serve this recipe, just as they do at Ury, with Keralan parathas (see page 132).

PREP TIME: 10 MINS
COOKING TIME: 15 MINS

- 2 tbsp coconut oil
- 1 tsp black mustard seeds
- 1 tbsp white split urad dhal lentils
- 2 heaped tbsp julienned ginger (more or less to taste)
- 20 curry leaves
- 1 onion, finely sliced, then cut into roughly 2.5cm (1in) pieces
- ½ tsp ground turmeric
- A handful of julienned carrot
- ½ coconut (fresh or frozen), grated
- 200g (7oz) julienned cabbage
- Salt and freshly ground black pepper

Heat the oil over medium–high heat and add the mustard seeds. When they begin to pop, add the lentils. Toast the lentils in the oil until they begin to turn light brown, about 30 seconds, then add the julienned ginger and curry leaves. Continue frying for another 30 seconds or until browned. Stir in the sliced onion and fry for about 5 minutes, until soft and translucent.

Now add the turmeric and julienned carrot followed by the coconut and give it all a good stir. To finish, add the cabbage and fry until cooked through. About 5 minutes should be enough. Season with salt and pepper to taste and serve immediately.

OKRA FRIES

SERVES 2 OR MORE AS PART OF A MULTI-COURSE MEAL

These okra fries always go down a treat. When I tried them for the first time, I was hooked. You can serve them with whatever sounds good. I like mine with hot sauce but ketchup is also a good and easy option.

PREP TIME: 10 MINS
COOKING TIME: 8 MINS

250g (9oz) okra
115g (1 cup) gram (chickpea) flour
1 tbsp rice flour
¼ tsp ajwain (carom) seeds (optional)
½ tsp ground turmeric
1 tsp chilli powder
½ tsp ground black pepper
½ tsp amchoor (dried mango powder)
½ tsp ground cumin
½ tsp ground coriander
Oil, for deep-frying
Salt
Sauce of your choice, to serve

Trim both ends off the okra. If you prefer longer fries, leave them as they are, or cut the okra in half for shorter pieces. Slice down the centre of each okra and scrape out all the seeds. Then cut them into thinner slices.

Make a slurry by whisking 8 tablespoons of the gram (chickpea) flour with 250ml (1 cup) water until there are no lumps.

Combine the remaining gram flour with the rice flour and all the spices (not the salt) in a large bowl, mixing everything together well. Set aside.

Heat about 10cm (4in) of oil in a large pan or wok over high heat. Your oil is ready when a small piece of okra sizzles and floats to the top immediately after placing it in the oil.

Dip the okra pieces in the slurry, then dust with the flour and spice mixture. Depending on the size of your pan, you will probably want to fry the okra in batches. Don't overcrowd your pan! Fry each batch for about 3 minutes, until crispy and brown. Transfer to paper towel to soak up excess oil and keep warm while you cook the remaining okra.

Sprinkle with salt to taste and serve with your preferred sauce.

CHICKPEA FRIES

SERVES 4 OR MORE AS PART OF A MULTI-COURSE MEAL

The first time I made chickpea (garbanzo bean) fries for my family, my daughters and wife went crazy for them. In fact, they prefer them to potato fries now. These are light in the centre and so nice and crispy on the exterior. My daughters now make and serve them with ketchup. Is that wrong?

PREP TIME: 5 MINS, PLUS CHILLING TIME
COOKING TIME: 20 MINS

2 tbsp ground cumin
1 tsp salt, plus extra to sprinkle
250g (2 cups) gram (chickpea) flour
Oil, for deep-frying
Chilli powder, to taste
Lemon wedges, to serve

Bring 1 litre (4 cups) water to a boil and add the cumin and salt. Stir in the gram (chickpea) flour and simmer while whisking constantly for about 3–4 minutes. You need to really whisk well to get all the lumps out. When ready, it should look like wet polenta.

Lay a sheet of greaseproof (wax) paper on a baking tray. Pour the gram flour mixture onto the lined tray and spread it out so that it is smooth on top and of equal thickness. Cover with cling film (plastic wrap) and place in the fridge for about 30 minutes to harden. After it has cooled, remove from the fridge and cut into fries.

Heat your oil for deep-frying. I usually use about 10cm (4in) of oil. Fry in batches for about 4–5 minutes, until nicely browned and crispy. Transfer to paper towel to soak up any excess oil and keep warm while you cook the remaining fries.

Serve sprinkled with chilli powder and a little more salt and with lemon wedges on the side.

KERALAN MASOOR DHAL WITH COCONUT

SERVES 4 OR MORE AS PART OF A MULTI-COURSE MEAL

I have given this popular dhal a south Indian touch using thick coconut milk and curry leaves. It is quick and easy to prepare and is great either on its own or served over rice.

PREP TIME 10 MINS, PLUS SOAKING TIME
COOKING TIME: 25 MINS

200g (1 cup) masoor dhal, rinsed and soaked in water for 10 mins
½ tsp ground turmeric
200ml (generous ¾ cup) thick coconut milk
Salt
3 tbsp finely chopped coriander (cilantro)

FOR THE TARKA
4 tbsp rapeseed (canola) or coconut oil
1 tsp black mustard seeds
1 tsp cumin seeds
10 curry leaves
3 dried Kashmiri chillies, deseeded, broken into pieces
1 red onion, finely chopped
5 garlic cloves, finely sliced
1–3 green chillies (to taste), finely chopped

Cover the masoor lentils with fresh water in a saucepan and simmer over medium–high heat until soft, about 20 minutes. Skim off any foam.

While the lentils are cooking, make the tarka. Heat the oil in a small frying pan over medium–high heat. When visibly hot, add the mustard seeds. When they begin to pop, stir in the cumin seeds, curry leaves and Kashmiri chillies. Allow to sizzle for about 30 seconds, then add the onion. Fry the onion until translucent and soft, about 5 minutes. Add the garlic and green chillies and cook until the garlic is softened, about 3 minutes. Be careful not to burn it or it will become bitter.

Once the dhal is cooked, add the turmeric and coconut milk and simmer for a further 5 minutes.

Pour the tarka mixture over the top, then season with salt to taste and garnish with the chopped coriander (cilantro).

GARLIC AND SPINACH DHAL

SERVES 4 OR MORE AS PART OF A MULTI-COURSE MEAL

Garlic, spinach and dhal are the perfect combo. If you're a big garlic fan, like me, go ahead and use more than I suggest below.

PREP TIME: 10 MINS, PLUS SOAKING TIME
COOKING TIME: 40 MINS

200g (1 cup) toor dhal
200g (1 cup) split yellow moong dhal
1 tsp ground turmeric
Salt
4 tbsp finely chopped coriander (cilantro), to serve
½ tsp garam masala, to serve

FOR THE TARKA
3 tbsp ghee, rapeseed (canola) or coconut oil
1 tsp black mustard seeds
1 tsp cumin seeds
10 curry leaves
1 large onion, finely chopped
3–4 green chillies, finely chopped
6 garlic cloves, finely minced
2.5cm (1in) piece of ginger, finely minced
3 tomatoes, diced
250g (9oz) frozen spinach or 500g (1lb 2oz) fresh
1 tsp ground turmeric
1 tsp chilli powder

Soak and rinse your dhals as per the packet instructions, then boil and simmer them with the turmeric until soft, about 30–40 minutes. Skim off any foam when cooking and add water if needed.

To make the tarka, heat the ghee or oil in a large frying pan over medium–high heat. When visibly hot, stir in the mustard seeds. When they begin to pop, add the cumin seeds and curry leaves and sizzle for about 30 seconds. Add the chopped onion and chillies and fry for 2 minutes, then stir in the garlic and ginger and fry for another 2 minutes, until the garlic is turning brown but not burnt. Add the tomatoes, spinach, turmeric and chilli powder and simmer until the spinach cooks down and turns darker, about 3 minutes.

Pour the tarka over the dhal and stir it in. Add salt to taste, then top with coriander (cilantro) and a little garam masala to serve.

CHANA DHAL CHUTNEY

SERVES 4 OR MORE

This might be one of my favourite chutneys. It's delicious served with dosas and idlis.

PREP TIME: 10 MINS
COOKING TIME: 15 MINS

2 tbsp rapeseed (canola) or coconut oil
5 tbsp chana dhal
3 dried red chillies
2.5cm (1in) piece of ginger, finely chopped
1 small tomato, roughly chopped
1 onion, finely chopped
25g (¼ cup) grated coconut (fresh or frozen)
¼ tsp asafoetida*
Salt

FOR THE TARKA
2 tbsp rapeseed (canola) or coconut oil
½ tsp black mustard seeds
10 fresh or frozen curry leaves

For the chutney, heat the oil in a large frying pan over medium–high heat. When hot, add the chana dhal and fry, stirring regularly until the dhal become fragrant and a nice golden brown. About about 1½–2 minutes should do. Transfer to a dish to cool.

Add the dried chillies, ginger, tomato, onion, coconut and asafoetida to the same pan and fry for about 5 minutes, until the tomato is mushy and the onion translucent and soft. Transfer this mixture and the roasted chana mixture to a spice grinder and grind until you have a smooth paste. Spoon it all into a serving bowl.

To make the tarka, heat the oil over high heat. When visibly hot, add the mustard seeds. When they begin to pop, stir in the curry leaves and fry for a further 30 seconds or so.

Pour this all over the chana chutney and season with salt to taste. Serve warm or cold.

NOTE
*If you are gluten-free, please check the asafoetida packaging as some brands contain wheat flour.

SESAME SEED AND CORIANDER CHUTNEY

MAKES 200ML (HEAPED ¾ CUP)

This simple chutney can be made in under ten minutes and keeps well in the fridge for about three days. I like to serve it with dosas and idlis but you could also add a tablespoon or so to your favourite curry.

PREP TIME: 5 MINS
COOKING TIME: 5 MINS

100g (¾ cup) sesame seeds
1 small bunch coriander (cilantro), chopped
1 green chilli, chopped
Juice of 1 lemon
3–4 garlic cloves, smashed
1 tbsp vegetable oil
A pinch of asafoetida*
Salt

Place the sesame seeds in a dry frying pan over medium heat. Stir regularly and fry for about 30–60 seconds, until the seeds are lightly browned. Transfer to a spice grinder and add the coriander (cilantro), chilli, lemon juice and garlic cloves, along with just enough water to blend. Blitz to a rough paste, making sure that it's not totally smooth and there is still a bit of texture. Season with salt.

Pour the oil into a frying pan over medium–high heat and stir in the asafoetida. Let it sizzle until it becomes quite fragrant. About 30 seconds should do.

Pour the oil over the blended ingredients and stir it in to serve.

NOTE
*If you are gluten-free, please check the asafoetida packaging as some brands contain wheat flour.

TOMATO, ONION AND YOGHURT SALAD

MAKES 500ML (2 CUPS)

You might think a soupy salad would be strange but you've got to try this. It's great on its own, poured over kebabs or with fresh naans. It is pictured on page 20.

PREP TIME: 10 MINS
COOKING TIME: 10 MINS

3 fresh tomatoes
3 garlic cloves in their skins
1 onion, finely chopped
1 green chilli, finely chopped
2 tbsp finely chopped coriander (cilantro)
2 tbsp mustard oil
A pinch of salt
A pinch of chaat masala, plus extra to serve
Juice of ½ lemon
2 tbsp plain yoghurt

Under the grill (broiler), roast the tomatoes whole until the skins are almost black, about 3–5 minutes. Do the same with the garlic cloves, roasting for about 3–5 minutes. If you have a gas stove, you might like to hold the cloves over an open flame on a fork and roast until the skins are blackened and the cloves are soft. Set the tomatoes and the garlic aside to cool, then finely chop them with or without the charred skins. I often leave the skins on.

Mix together the onion, green chilli, coriander (cilantro), mustard oil, salt and chaat masala. Squeeze in the lemon juice.

Now mix in the garlic and tomatoes by hand, ensuring the garlic cloves are crushed and the tomatoes are slushy. You can either remove the tomato skin at this stage or leave it in. I leave it on. Add the yoghurt and stir well.

The salad should be served chilled with a little more chaat masala sprinkled over the top.

MAKE IT VEGAN
Use vegan yoghurt in place of the plain yoghurt.

TOMATO, ONION AND MINT SALAD

SERVES 4 OR MORE

This simple salad (shown on page 115) makes a perfect side for your summer barbecue.

PREP TIME: 10 MINS, PLUS STANDING TIME

5 tennis-ball sized firm tomatoes, thinly sliced
1 onion, thinly sliced
2 green chilli peppers, finely chopped (optional)
1 tbsp mint sauce
2 tbsp finely chopped coriander (cilantro)
Juice and finely grated zest of 1 lime or lemon
Salt and freshly ground black pepper

Mix together all of the ingredients and season with salt and pepper to taste. Allow to sit for 15 minutes before serving.

MINT RAITA

SERVES 4 OR MORE
MAKES 320ML (1⅓ CUPS)

This curry-house-style mint raita is possibly the most requested recipe I get. It is pictured on page 87.

PREP TIME: 5 MINS

300g (1¼ cups) Greek yoghurt
2 tbsp mint sauce
1 tsp sugar
½ tsp roasted cumin seeds
2 tbsp finely chopped coriander (cilantro)
A splash of milk, if needed
Salt

Whisk all the ingredients together except the milk. Adjust to taste, adding salt and more sugar or mint sauce if needed. If you prefer it thinner, stir in milk, 1 tablespoon at a time, until right.

MAKE IT VEGAN
Use whisked vegan yoghurt in place of the Greek yoghurt and omit the milk.

RED DIPPING SAUCE

SERVES 4 OR MORE

I'm always asked for 'that red dipping sauce' you get at curry houses. So here you go!

PREP TIME: 5 MINS

150ml (scant ⅔ cup) pineapple juice
150ml (scant ⅔ cup) tomato ketchup
150ml (scant ⅔ cup) mango chutney
3–5 tbsp mint sauce (the vinegar in mint sauce is the sour part of the 'sweet and sour'. Add it to your own taste)
1 tsp dried fenugreek leaves (kasoori methi)
1 tbsp tandoori masala (shop-bought is fine)
red food colouring (optional)
Salt

Mix the pineapple juice, ketchup, mango chutney, mint sauce, fenugreek leaves (kasoori methi) and tandoori masala together. Add just enough red food colouring, if using, to give it that recognizable red glow. Season with salt to taste.

SPICY CASHEW DIP

MAKES 200ML (HEAPED ¾ CUP)

This is delicious with papadams and naan or used as a sauce for sandwiches or wraps.

PREP TIME: 3 MINS

150g (1¼ cups) raw cashews
2 garlic cloves
1 tsp toasted cumin seeds
½ tsp chilli powder
Juice of 2 limes, plus extra if needed
Salt

Place the cashews and garlic in a blender with 100ml (scant ½ cup) water and blend to a thick paste. Stir in the cumin seeds, chilli powder and lime juice. The lime juice will thin the dip. If you want it even thinner, add more lime juice or water.

Season with salt to taste and serve.

COCONUT AND CHILLI SAMBOL

MAKES ABOUT 500ML (2 CUPS)

This chutney is great with hoppers (see page 96) as well as with dosas and idlis. It can be made in a food processor but it is better hand-ground. It is pictured on page 87.

PREP TIME: 20 MINS

3 red chilli peppers, roughly chopped
½ tsp salt (or to taste)
Shredded flesh from 1 coconut
1 red onion, roughly chopped
Juice of 1–2 limes

Using a pestle and mortar or a grinding stone, start by grinding the chilli and salt to a paste with a splash of water. Add the coconut and onion and keep grinding until you have a chunky, thick paste. Add lime juice to taste and serve.

PICKLED RED ONION

SERVES 2–4

Pickled red onions not only taste great, but they also look great as a garnish.

PREP TIME: 2 MINS, PLUS PICKLING TIME
COOKING TIME: 5 MINS

1 tsp salt
1 tsp sugar
125ml (½ cup) white vinegar
1 red onion, peeled and finely sliced
1 green chilli, sliced lengthwise

Bring 125ml (½ cup) water to a simmer and stir in the salt and sugar. Stir until it is all dissolved. Turn off the heat and allow to cool. Stir in the vinegar.

Place your onions and chilli in a bowl or glass jar and top with the vinegar mixture. Allow to pickle for at least an hour but ideally a few hours.

Store, covered, in the fridge. For optimum flavour and texture, use within a week. The pickling liquid can be used over and over again.

Top, from left to right: Neer dosa (see page 85); beetroot thoran (page 117); spicy mixed vegetable pickle (page 128); spinach and sweetcorn (page 117); smoked toor dhal samosas (page 19); papadam (page 14); masala plantain chips (page 22)
Bottom: Coconut rice (page 141); tinda masala (page 51); Keralan massoor dhal with coconut (page 122); mango pickle (page 127); spicy cashew dip (page 125)

GARLIC PICKLE

MAKES: 250ML (1 CUP)

This pickle is best made with older garlic, with loose paper-like skin, as it is less likely to turn green than young, fresh garlic. It is still edible when it turns green but it doesn't look as attractive. As you will probably keep this pickle for at least a few weeks, older garlic is the way to go for presentation reasons.

PREP TIME: 15 MINS, PLUS PICKLING TIME
COOKING TIME: 15 MINS

4 tbsp mustard oil
30 old garlic cloves, cut into small pieces
½ tsp ground turmeric
¼ tsp asafoetida (please be aware that some brands may contain gluten)
3 tbsp lemon or lime juice
1 tsp sugar
1 tbsp chilli powder (more or less to taste)
¼ tsp fenugreek (methi) seeds
2 tsp black mustard seeds
½ tsp cumin seeds
½ tsp coriander seeds
1 tbsp salt
Rapeseed (canola) oil, to top up

Heat the oil over medium–high heat in a large frying pan until it begins to smoke. Turn off the heat and allow to cool. Then heat it back up again and fry the garlic, stirring continuously, for about 5 minutes, until soft. Add the turmeric and asafoetida and sizzle in the oil for 30 seconds before squeezing in the lemon or lime juice. Stir in the sugar and chilli powder and fry for another 2–3 minutes, until the sugar has dissolved.

Now place the fenugreek (methi) seeds, mustard seeds, cumin seeds and coriander seeds in a pestle and mortar and crush lightly. This shouldn't be a fine powder, but a powder all the same.

Remove the garlic mixture from the heat and stir in the crushed spices and salt. Mix it all up really well and decant it into a sterilized jar (see 'Storing Pickles' on page 7). Store for at least a week before serving and keep it in the fridge once opened. I recommend topping it up with some oil before storing, which will help preserve the pickle.

MANGO PICKLE

MAKES: A 1 LITRE (1 QUART) JAR

This is one of my most popular pickles. It's so good and really unique in flavour too. You can see it pictured on page 15.

PREP TIME: 15 MINS, PLUS PICKLING TIME
COOKING TIME: 5 MINS

5 green mangos, pitted and cut into bite-sized pieces
1 tsp salt
1 tsp ground turmeric
Juice of 3 limes
1 tbsp cumin seeds
1 tbsp coriander seeds
2.5cm (1in) piece of ginger, peeled and cut into slivers
4 tbsp garlic purée
2 tsp red chilli powder (or more to taste)

FOR THE TEMPERING
450ml (scant 2 cups) sesame oil
1 tbsp brown mustard seeds
10 fenugreek (methi) seeds
1 tsp nigella (onion) seeds
6 dried long red chillies
15 cloves garlic

Place the mangos, salt and turmeric in a large glass jar with a tight-fitting lid. Mix well, then partially cover and allow to sit for 3 days. The mango needs a little air, so leave a small gap. Stir the pickle once or twice each day.

On the third day, add the lime juice and stir again. Leave for one more day.

On the fourth day, add the cumin seeds, coriander seeds, ginger, garlic purée and chilli powder. Stir well.

To temper, heat the sesame oil in a large pan over medium heat. When hot, add the rest of the tempering ingredients and fry for about 2 minutes. Be careful not to burn the garlic. Remove the oil from the heat and allow to cool.

When cool, pour the oil and spices into the mango mixture and stir very well to completely coat the mango pieces. Cover the pickle with a lid.

Let the mango pickle sit for 4 days in a tightly covered jar or bowl. Stir twice daily.

Scoop the mixture into air-tight sterilized jars (see page 7) and let it mature for about a week before eating. Store in the fridge after opening.

SPICY MIXED VEGETABLE PICKLE

MAKES: A 1 LITRE (1 QUART) JAR

I always have some of this mixed pickle on hand just in case I get unexpected guests. It is one of my favourites and goes well with everything from papadams to dosas. You can vary the vegetables you use depending on what sounds good and is in season. I've used marrow, radishes, turnips, broccoli and even pumpkin in the past with excellent results. I like my pickles to be quite spicy. If you don't, reduce the amount of chillies and chilli powder. You can always add more to taste later.

PREP TIME: 15 MINS, PLUS PICKLING TIME
COOKING TIME: 20 MINS

- 150g (5½oz) cauliflower, cut into small pieces
- 100g (1 cup) diced aubergine (eggplant)
- 1 small carrot, cut into small pieces
- 1 red (bell) pepper, roughly chopped
- 3 green chillies, thinly sliced
- 1 mango, peeled, pitted and diced
- 6 garlic cloves
- 3 limes, thoroughly washed
- 1 tbsp black mustard seeds
- 3 tbsp chilli powder
- 1 tsp ground turmeric
- ½ tsp ground fenugreek (methi)
- 3 tbsp flaky sea salt

FOR THE TARKA

- 125ml (½ cup) rapeseed (canola) oil, plus extra if needed
- 2 tsp black mustard seeds
- 1 tsp cumin seeds
- 2 dried Kashmiri chillies, broken into three pieces each
- 10 curry leaves, finely chopped

Mix all the chopped vegetables, chillies, mango and garlic in a glass or ceramic mixing bowl. Quarter the limes and squeeze as much of the juice out of them as you can over the ingredients.

Heat some water in a pan with a steamer basket and steam the squeezed lime quarters as they are for about 15 minutes to soften them. You can add the steamed lime quarters as they are to the bowl or cut them into even smaller pieces before adding.

Using a pestle and mortar, grind the 1 tablespoon of black mustard seeds to a coarse powder. Pour this powder, along with the chilli powder, turmeric, fenugreek (methi) and salt over the vegetables and fruit in the bowl. Stir well to combine.

Now, in a small frying pan, bring about 3 tablespoons of the tarka oil to a bubble over high heat. Add the mustard seeds. When they begin to pop, reduce the temperature to medium–high and stir in the cumin seeds, Kashmiri chillies and curry leaves. When these become fragrant – about 30 seconds should do – pour in the remaining oil, stir well and pour it all over the chopped vegetables and fruit.

Mix really well. The vegetables and fruit should be submerged in the oil. If not, add a little more and then cover with cling film (plastic wrap).

In the summer months, you can place this outside in the sun. In colder months, place it all by a sunny window. Leave to ferment for 3 days, stirring every 8 hours or so. Then scoop it all into a sterilized jar (see 'Storing Pickles' on page 7) with a tight-fitting lid. You can taste it now but wait for at least a week if you can. It gets better!

This pickle will keep in the fridge for at least 3 months. Make sure that the vegetables and fruit are always covered in oil to avoid it going off.

RED COCONUT CHUTNEY

MAKES ABOUT 250ML (1 CUP)

This chutney is so good as an accompaniment for dosas and idlis. It is similar to the green chutney (right) but is a deeper heat and is slightly tangier. If you don't want to break into a coconut and grate it, you could use frozen shredded coconut or even coconut flakes. If using dried flakes, rinse and soak them in 250ml (1 cup) water for about 30 minutes before starting this recipe.

PREP TIME: 10 MINS
COOKING TIME: 2 MINS

4 heaped tbsp chana dhal
100g (1 cup) grated fresh or frozen coconut
3 dried Kasmiri chillies
1½ tbsp garlic and ginger paste
1½ tsp tamarind concentrate or tamarind sauce (see page 10)
Salt

FOR THE TEMPERING
2 tbsp coconut or rapeseed (canola) oil
1 tsp mustard seeds
1 tsp cumin seeds
A pinch (¼ tsp) asafoetida (please be aware that some brands may contain gluten)
6–10 fresh or frozen curry leaves

Toast the chana dhal in a dry frying pan over medium–high heat until fragrant and lightly browned, about 1½–2 minutes. Transfer to a plate to cool slightly.

Place the chana dhal, coconut, Kashmiri chillies, garlic and ginger paste, tamarind and 125ml (½ cup) water in a spice grinder or blender and blend to a paste. This chutney should be quite thin, so stir in more water until you are happy with the consistency. Try some and add salt to taste.

Now heat the oil in a small pan over high heat. When visibly hot, pour in the mustard seeds. When they begin to pop, lower the heat to medium–high and add the cumin seeds, asafoetida and curry leaves. Move these ingredients around in the oil until the beautiful aroma fills your kitchen – about 30 seconds should do. Pour it all over the chutney to serve.

GREEN COCONUT CHUTNEY

MAKES ABOUT 300ML (1¼ CUPS)

I can't get enough of this mildly spiced chutney (pictured on page 15)!

PREP TIME: 10 MINS, PLUS SOAKING TIME IF USING DRIED COCONUT FLAKES
COOKING TIME: 2 MINS

4 tbsp chana dhal
100g (1 cup) grated fresh coconut, frozen shredded coconut or dried coconut flakes (see recipe introduction to the left if using dried)
40g (¾ cup) coriander (cilantro)
2 green chillies, roughly chopped
2cm (¾in) piece of ginger, peeled and roughly chopped
¼ tsp sugar (or to taste)
Juice of ½ lemon
Salt

FOR THE TEMPERING
1 tbsp coconut or rapeseed (canola) oil
½ tsp mustard seeds
½ tsp white split urad dhal lentils
¼ tsp asafoetida (please be aware that some brands may contain gluten)
4–5 curry leaves

Toast the chana dhal in a dry frying pan over medium–high heat until fragrant and lightly browned, about 1½–2 minutes. Transfer to a plate to cool slightly.

Put the coconut, coriander (cilantro), green chillies, ginger and toasted chana dhal in a blender or spice grinder and blend with 125ml (½ cup) water. This is a runny chutney so add more water until the consistency is right. Add the sugar, lemon juice and salt to taste.

Heat the oil in a small pan over high heat. When hot, add the mustard seeds. When they begin to pop, lower the temperature to medium–high and stir in the white urad dhal. Let the dhal toast until light brown – about a minute should do. Stir in the asafoetida and curry leaves and let this all sizzle in the oil for about 20 seconds. Your kitchen will smell amazing.

Pour the spiced oil over the chutney to serve.

BREAD AND RICE

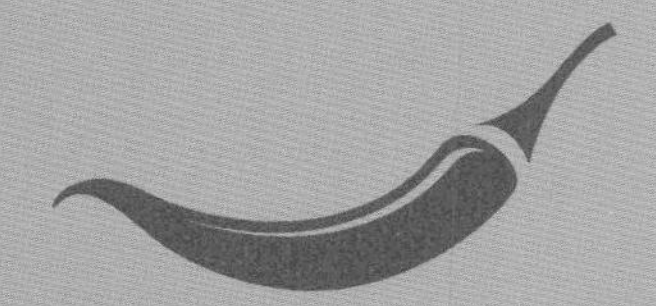

Naans, chapattis, puris... they're all here, but I've gone a bit further with this section to bring you some of the other, hugely popular bread recipes that are making their way on to the best menus. You can't beat fried bread, so try the katlamas on page 136. You'll be happy you did. Have you ever tried dhoklas? If not, be sure to check out page 135. My favourite bread at southern Indian restaurants is Keralan paratha (see page 132). This takes some work but the time is well spent as they are certain to get gobbled up!

We all like a good rice side dish, and you'll find some delicious recipes for those, too, in the following pages.

GARLIC NAANS

MAKES 6 LARGE

In my first two cookbooks, I included recipes for naans the way I have seen them done most often. This is a recipe that doesn't include milk, yoghurt or eggs. It's simple but works every time with outstanding results. The dough is also good used as a pizza base, as I do on pages 112 and 114.

PREP TIME: 25 MINS, PLUS RESTING TIME
COOKING TIME: 35 MINS

FOR THE NAAN DOUGH
- 600g (4½ cups) plain (all-purpose) white flour, plus more for rolling out
- 1 tbsp salt
- 1 tsp baking powder
- 7g (¼oz) dried yeast
- 2 tbsp sugar

FOR THE GARLIC BUTTER
- 4 tbsp melted butter or vegetable ghee
- 3 garlic cloves, finely chopped
- 3 tbsp chopped fresh coriander (cilantro)

Sift the flour, salt and baking powder into a large mixing bowl. Set aside.

Bring 210ml (scant 1 cup) water to a rapid boil. Pour it into a jug and top with 210ml (scant 1 cup) cold water. This should be the perfect temperature to wake up the dried yeast. Stir in the yeast and sugar and leave to froth up for about 10 minutes.

When the yeast water is nice and bubbly, make a well in the flour mixture and pour it into the well. Mix it all together with your hands for a minute or so, then leave to rest for 2 minutes. Then knead the dough as best you can for about 5 minutes. It will be very sticky but don't be tempted to add more flour. Form into a ball, cover and leave to rise for an hour in a warm place.

When the dough has risen (it should double in size, but don't worry if it doesn't) divide it into six equal-sized pieces. Dust each with a little flour and form into smooth balls. Place on a high-sided tray and cover with a clean tea (dish) towel. Let the dough balls rise for another hour.

When I cook in a tandoor, I place the balls on a floured surface and work them out into naan shapes with oiled hands. When pan frying, I just use flour.

Roll each ball out into a round or teardrop shape. For crispy naans, roll them quite thin. For fluffier naans, the discs should be about 5mm (¼in) thick.

Heat a heavy-based pan, preferably cast iron, over high heat until the base of the pan is extremely hot. Think tandoor here! Slap the naan discs around between your hands to remove any excess flour.

If using an electric hob, fry on the first side until bubbles begin to form on the top. Then flip it over briefly to brown the other side.

If using a gas hob, wet one side of the naan with water and then slap it down hard on the pan, water-side down. The naan should stick to the pan. Fry until bubbles form on top. Turn the pan over so that the gas flame browns the top. Gravity will make the bubbles larger and you will have a naan that looks just like it came out of the tandoor. Pry the naan off the pan with a metal spatula or similar. Repeat with the other naans, then wrap in foil to keep warm.

While the naans are cooking, combine the melted butter or vegetable ghee with the chopped garlic and coriander (cilantro).

To serve, brush each naan with the flavoured butter.

KERALAN PARATHAS
(FRIED LAYERED UNLEAVENED FLATBREAD)

MAKES 6

Keralan parathas take some practice to get right, but even if yours don't look great at first, they will still taste delicious! It took me some time until I was completely happy with mine and I've enjoyed eating and serving my failed attempts. Just go for it and have fun. The preparation time is quite long, but you will get much faster if you make these often. If you would like to watch me make them, I've made a video on my YouTube channel, Dan Toombs.

PREP TIME: 60 MINS, PLUS RESTING TIME
COOKING TIME: 20 MINS

450g (3 cups) plain (all-purpose) flour
80g (½ cup) semolina flour
1 tsp salt
3 tbsp sugar
Around 50g (3½ tbsp) melted, warm ghee, vegetable ghee or rapeseed (canola) oil
Oil, for greasing

Pour the flours, salt and sugar into a large mixing bowl. Slowly drizzle in 300ml (1¼ cups) warm water while working the dough with your hands into a soft but firm, easy-to-handle dough. Kneed for 5 minutes, then cover and allow to rest for 20 minutes, or even overnight.

Dip your fingers in the ghee or oil and work the dough into 6 equal-sized balls. The ghee or oil makes working with the dough easier, plus adds flavour. Let the dough balls rest, covered, for another 5 minutes.

Lightly oil your work surface and place one of the dough balls on top. Flatten it with your hands, then roll out into a large rectangular shape. The dough needs to be really thin so that your parathas are nice and flaky. You should be able to see the surface through it.

With the longest sides at the top and bottom, use a sharp knife to cut slits across the width of the dough at about 5mm (¼in) intervals but leaving the edges intact, so that the dough is still joined at the sides. Lightly brush all over the surface with a little ghee or oil.

Now carefully begin to roll the dough up from the bottom into a long sausage. This will be difficult because of the slits so I find that using a sharp knife to help lift the dough from the surface helps. Once you have a long dough rope, curl that up into a spiral, so it looks like a Chelsea bun or cinnamon roll. The idea here is to get as many layers in your paratha as possible. Repeat to roll up all the dough pieces in the same way. Let each ball sit for at least 5 minutes, covered.

Flatten one of the parathas with your hands, until it is about 18cm (7in) in diameter. Be careful not to press down too hard or you will lose some of those layers. The swirls should be visible at the top.

Melt a little ghee or oil in a non-stick pan over medium heat. Place your paratha in the pan, cook for about 30 seconds, then flip it over. You can start flattening your next paratha while this one is cooking. Continue cooking the first paratha, flipping regularly so it doesn't burn, until it is cooked through and browned on both sides – about 3–5 minutes. Flatten and cook the rest of the parathas, stacking the cooked ones as you make them and keeping them warm under a cloth.

Once they are all cooked, bash the stack of parathas lightly with your hands on the sides so the layers become more visible, then serve.

PURIS

(UNLEAVENED PUFFED FRIED BREAD)

MAKES 6

I am hooked on puris! Especially served for breakfast with the potato curry on page 74. You will see my finished puris on that page too. There is really so much you can do with puris. Dip them into curries and dhals, or they are delicious served with pickles, like the spicy mixed vegetable pickle on page 128. At the end of the day, these are fried bread so I'm sure you'll find a use for them.

PREP TIME: 20 MINS, PLUS RESTING TIME
COOKING TIME: 10 MINS

450g (3¼ cups) chapatti flour, plus extra for dusting
A pinch of salt
Oil, for deep-frying

Sift the chapatti flour into a large bowl with the salt. Slowly add about 250ml (1 cup) warm water until you have a soft, pliable dough. Knead the dough for about 10 minutes, then set aside, covered with a tea (dish) towel, for about 30 minutes.

Divide the dough into six equal-sized balls. Using a rolling pin, roll out the small dough balls on a floured surface until round and quite flat. Try to keep them as perfectly round as possible for best results.

Heat about 10cm (4in) of the oil in a large wok. When a piece of rolled-out puri sizzles instantly when hitting the oil, you're ready to fry. If you have an oil thermometer, you're aiming for 190°C (375°F). Don't overcrowd your pan – cook one puri at a time if necessary. Slowly lower the flat puris into the oil and deep-fry for 30 seconds, until the puris puff up and are light brown in colour. Tapping them lightly with the back of your spatula will help them balloon up. They are ready when lightly browned. If they are not cooked enough, they will deflate when you take them out of the oil. I usually turn my puris in the oil at least once to cook both sides evenly.

Carefully remove them with a slotted spoon or spider strainer when ready and rest on paper towels to absorb any excess oil.

You can serve puris on their own, as you would naans, or filled with the filling of your choice. Serve immediately.

DHOKLAS (FLUFFY GRAM FLOUR AND YOGHURT STEAMED BREAD)

SERVES 4 OR MORE AS PART OF A MULTI-COURSE MEAL

If you've never tried dhoklas, it's time you did. They can be eaten hot or cold and are bursting with so many amazing flavours. They are fluffy, cake-like and taste slightly sweet and a little savoury. I had the pleasure of trying my first dhokla at an Indian savoury shop on Brick Lane in London and I made it my goal to learn how to make them. This recipe will get you started but it doesn't make a huge amount. In fact it only makes about 300ml (just over a cup) of batter, so you will need a small tray to steam it in. You can easily scale the recipe up if you would like to make these for a crowd. My bet is that you will! You can see my finished dhoklas next to the hasselback butternut squash on page 110.

PREP TIME: 10 MINS
COOKING TIME: 12 MINS

- 130g (1 cup) gram (chickpea) flour
- 2 tbsp fine semolina
- 1 generous tbsp sugar
- 1 tsp salt
- 2 tsp baking powder
- ¾ tsp citric acid powder or the juice of 1 lemon
- 1 heaped tbsp ginger paste
- 2–3 green chillies, finely chopped
- ½ tsp ground turmeric
- ¼ tsp chilli powder
- 3 tsp rapeseed (canola) oil
- 1 tsp black mustard seeds
- ½ tsp asafoetida*
- 1 tsp sesame seeds
- 10 fresh or frozen curry leaves
- 2 tbsp dried coconut flakes
- 2 tbsp finely chopped coriander (cilantro)

Sift the gram (chickpea) flour, semolina, sugar, salt, baking powder and citric acid powder or lemon juice into a large mixing bowl. Add the ginger paste, chopped green chillies, turmeric and chilli powder along with 250ml (1 cup) water and whisk until creamy smooth with no lumps.

Grease a dhokla tray or a deep small baking tray with 1 teaspoon of the oil and pour in the batter. Place the tray in a steamer over boiling water and cover. The tray should not be touching the boiling water. Steam for 15–17 minutes. You know it is ready when it feels like cake on the top and when you stick a fork in and it comes out clean.

Remove from the steamer and let it sit for a few minutes, then cut around the edges and either lift out or turn it over onto a serving plate. You may need to help the dhokla out with a knife and/or spatula.

Heat the remaining 2 teaspoons of oil in a frying pan. When the oil is visibly hot, add the mustard seeds. When they begin to crackle, add the asafoetida, sesame seeds, curry leaves and coconut flakes. Allow to sizzle for about 30 seconds, until the coconut is nicely toasted. Add about 2 tablespoons of water to the tarka. This will help keep the dhoklas moist.

Pour this all over the dhokla and garnish with the chopped coriander (cilantro). Slice the dhokla into small bite-sized squares to serve.

NOTE

*If you are gluten-free, please check the asafoetida packaging as some brands contain wheat flour.

KATLAMAS
(DEEP-FRIED UNLEAVENED FLATBREAD)

SERVES 4

Who doesn't love fried bread? Katlamas are served at many Pakistani-run restaurants around the UK and elsewhere, so look out for them. This flavourful fried bread can be quite impressive. I've seen family-sized katlamas made in huge woks that are about 90cm (3ft) in diameter! That's for the professionals though, as they are quite difficult to handle. This recipe makes four smaller katlamas, but if you have a large wok or karahi and want to give the larger ones a try, go for it.

PREP TIME: 30 MINS, PLUS SOAKING AND RESTING TIME
COOKING TIME: 15 MINS

3 tbsp mung dhal
240g (2 cups) chapatti flour (or a 50/50 mix of white and wholewheat flour), plus extra for dusting
2 tbsp rapeseed (canola) oil, plus more for deep-frying
½ tsp salt
120g (1 cup) gram (chickpea) flour
1 tbsp chilli powder
1 egg, beaten
1 tsp ground cumin
1 tbsp pomegranate seeds
1 tbsp coriander seeds
2 green chillies, finely chopped
Sea salt flakes
Yoghurt sauce (see page 9), to serve

Soak the mung dhal overnight in water, then drain.

In a large mixing bowl, work the chapatti flour, rapeseed (canola) oil, salt and 500ml (2 cups) water into a firm but soft dough, and knead for about 5 minutes. Cover with a damp cloth and allow to rest for about 30 minutes.

Meanwhile, in another bowl, mix the gram (chickpea) flour, chilli powder, egg and cumin together. Pour in about 250ml (1 cup) water, a little at a time, until you have a gooey paste. It should ooze through your fingers when you pick it up. It shouldn't be too thin as you want to be able to spread it easily over the katlamas, not pour it. If you mistakenly add too much water, just add a little more gram flour to thicken it up again.

Now divide the dough into four equal-sized balls. Take one dough ball and roll it out on a lightly floured surface until it is about 25cm (10in) in diameter. Spread a quarter of the gram-flour mixture evenly over the surface and top with a quarter of the pomegranate seeds, coriander seeds, chillies and the mung dhal. Repeat with the remaining dough balls.

Heat about 10cm (4in) of oil in a wok or large pan. Depending on the shape of your pan, you might need to add a little more oil as the katlamas need to deep-fry in the oil. When a piece of dough instantly sizzles in the hot oil and rises to the top, you are ready to start frying.

Place one of the dough discs in the oil. It should instantly begin to bubble up. Press it down lightly with a spatula or spoon so that it fries evenly. After about 2 minutes, your katlama will be nicely browned and cooked through. With a slotted spoon or spatula, transfer it from the oil to a plate lined with paper towel to soak up any excess oil. Keep warm and repeat to cook the remaining katlamas.

Sprinkle with a little flaky sea salt and serve with yoghurt sauce.

MAKE IT VEGAN

You could leave the egg out of the paste, although you might need to adjust the amount of water used. Serve with a yoghurt sauce made with soy or coconut yoghurt or whatever else you wish.

BEETROOT CHAPATTIS
(UNLEAVENED FLATBREADS MADE WITH WHEAT FLOUR AND BEETROOT)

SERVES 4 OR MORE AS PART OF A MULTI-COURSE MEAL

The beetroot gives these chapattis an eye-pleasing red colour that I really like. When cooked, they taste like normal chapattis as you really can't taste the beetroot. These chapattis can be seen on page 39, used for the runner bean wraps. In that recipe, I cut them quite small as it is a starter, but you can, of course, roll your chapattis out as small or as large as you like them.

PREP TIME: 20 MINS, PLUS RESTING TIME
COOKING TIME: 1 MIN PER CHAPATTI

1 beetroot
260g (2 cups) chapatti flour, plus extra for dusting
1 tbsp unsalted butter
1 tsp salt
½ tsp cumin seeds
1 tsp rapeseed (canola) oil

Peel and cut the beetroot into small pieces, then blend it with 125ml (½ cup) water into a smooth paste.

Mix the chapatti flour, butter, salt, cumin seeds and the blended beetroot in a bowl and knead it until you have a dough that is elastic but not at all sticky. This will take about 5–10 minutes. Rub the oil all over the ball and cover with a damp cloth to rest for 2 hours or overnight.

To make the chapattis, lightly flour a clean work surface. I normally roll the ball out into one large, thin sheet. Then I use a small round cookie cutter to cut out the chapattis so that they are all uniform in shape. Another way to do this is to divide the dough into lime-sized balls and roll them out into round chapattis.

When ready to cook, heat a large frying pan or tawa over medium–high heat and when hot, place your first chapatti in the pan. After about 15 seconds, small bubbles will begin to appear on top. Flip it over and cook the other side for about 20 seconds, then flip over again. Keep flipping until cooked through – about 1 minute per chapatti. You may see a few brown spots, which is okay.

Place the cooked chapattis in a bowl lined with a soft tea (dish) towel and cover while you make the rest of the chapattis. The steam from the cooked chapattis will keep them nice and soft to serve.

MAKE IT VEGAN

Substitute vegetable ghee or non-dairy butter for the butter.

RUMALI ROTIS
(SUPER-THIN UNLEAVENED FLATBREAD)

MAKES 8 SMALL OR 4 LARGE ROTIS (SERVES 4)

Rumali rotis, or handkerchief rotis as they are also known, are up there with my favourites. They are delicious served with a curry and are also good as a wrap for recipes like vegetable frankies (see page 42) and paneer kathi rolls (see page 44). The finished rotis are light and thinner than tortillas or chapattis. They are also fun to make. You will need a large wok and you'll be cooking the rotis on its underside. It is better to cook these on a gas hob, however if you have an electric or induction hob, or just want to make things easy, you could cook the rotis in a normal non-stick frying pan instead.

PREP TIME: 20 MINS, PLUS STANDING TIME
COOKING TIME: 15 MINS

- 250g (2 cups) plain (all-purpose) flour, plus extra for dusting
- 1½ tsp table salt, plus an extra 1 tbsp for cooking
- 2 tbsp rapeseed (canola) oil

Sift the flour into a large mixing bowl. Add the 1½ teaspoon salt and the oil, then slowly pour in 200ml (generous ¾ cup) warm water while working with your hands. Form into a soft dough and knead for at least 10 minutes on a flour-dusted surface. Return the dough ball to the bowl and cover with a damp cloth. Allow to sit for at least 20 minutes, but an hour would be even better.

When ready to cook, separate the dough into four large balls or eight small balls. Using a rolling pin, roll out each ball into a circle. You want the rotis to be as thin as you can get them. I like them large, for wrapping, and aim to roll four balls into 35cm (14in) or larger pancakes, but you can make smaller pancakes, for serving as light snacks.

Mix the 1 tablespoon salt with about 250ml (1 cup) water and stir well to dissolve the salt.

Heat a wok over high heat for about 2 minutes. When really hot, turn the wok upside down, still over the heat. You are going to cook the rotis on the underside of the wok. Splash the underside with some of the salt water. The salt will dry and help ensure the rotis don't stick.

Take your first roti and carefully place it on the salted surface. Allow it to cook for about 20 seconds. Bubbles will begin to rise on top. Flip it over and cook the other side for 20 seconds. Flip it over again and cook until light brown spots begin to appear on the underside. Flip it again and do the same on the other side until cooked through. Transfer to a plate and fold in half and then again into a little triangle. Be careful not to overcook or the thin, soft rotis will become hard. Cover with a cloth towel to keep warm while you cook the remaining rotis.

TAMARIND RICE

SERVES 2–3

This mildly spiced and tart tamarind rice is a good one! It is a nice way to use up leftover white rice while making it a lot more interesting. The finished dish is delicious as a side dish but it can also be served as a main. The runny paste for the sauce can be made ahead of time – it will keep for weeks in the fridge. All you need to do is add the cold, cooked rice and you've got yourself a rice dish that you will want to make again and again!

PREP TIME: 10 MINS, PLUS COOKING THE RICE IF NOT USING LEFTOVERS
COOKING TIME: 15 MINS

3 tbsp sesame seeds
2 tbsp rapeseed (canola) oil
1 tsp mustard seeds
1 tbsp chana dhal
½ tsp asafoetida*
10 curry leaves
3 tbsp raw peanuts
3 dried Kashmiri chillies
2 green chillies, finely chopped
½ tsp chilli powder
1 tsp ground coriander
1 tsp ground cumin
1 generous tbsp tamarind concentrate, or 3 tbsp tamarind sauce (see page 10)
400g (2 cups) cold, cooked Basmati rice
Salt

Toast the sesame seeds in a frying pan over medium heat until lightly browned and fragrant. Allow to cool slightly, then grind the sesame seeds to a fine powder in a spice grinder or pestle and mortar. Set aside.

Heat the oil in a large frying pan over medium–high heat. When visibly hot, add the mustard seeds. When they begin to pop, lower the heat to medium and add the chana dhal and asafoetida. Toast the chana until lightly browned, about 1½–2 minutes. Add the curry leaves, peanuts and dried Kashmiri chillies. The peanuts should cook through and become crunchier as they fry in the oil.

Stir in the sesame powder, green chillies, chilli powder, coriander and cumin and mix it all up. Add the tamarind concentrate or sauce and about 250ml (1 cup) water. Bring the water to a simmer, stirring regularly, and reduce it down until only about 5 tablespoons of water remain in the pan. At this stage, you could store the sauce in an air-tight container in the fridge until ready to use.

If using immediately, add the cooked rice and ensure that it is very well coated with the tamarind mixture. Keep cooking to heat the rice through. You want the rice to be very hot, so add a drop more water if it begins to stick. Be sure not to stir the rice too vigorously or it will turn to mush.

To finish, add salt to taste and serve immediately.

NOTES

If you are reheating cold, cooked rice, as in this recipe, it is important that you refrigerate the rice quickly after you first cook it. It is advised not to eat rice that has been sitting at room temperature for longer than 40 minutes. You should also make sure you use the rice within one day and thoroughly heat it through when reheating.

*If you are gluten-free, please check the asafoetida packaging as some brands contain wheat flour.

COCONUT RICE

SERVES 4 OR MORE AS PART OF A MULTI-COURSE MEAL

The perfect one-pot dish! I must cook this coconut rice weekly. It's so simple to make and the ingredients work so well together. This is one you could seriously serve on its own, but if you've ever had it at a south Indian restaurant, you'll know it makes a delicious side for almost any curry.

PREP TIME: 10 MINS, PLUS SOAKING TIME
COOKING TIME: 50 MINS

370g (2 cups) Basmati rice
3 tbsp coconut oil or ghee
1 tsp mustard seeds
1 tsp chana dhal
1 tsp white split urad dhal lentils
1.25cm (½in) piece of cinnamon stick
4 cardamom pods, smashed
10 curry leaves
2 dried red chillies
2 green chillies, cut lengthwise
4 tbsp coconut flakes (optional)
200ml (generous ¾ cup) thick coconut milk
Salt

Rinse the rice in several changes of cold water until the water runs almost clear. Cover with clean water and allow to soak for 30 minutes.

Meanwhile, melt the coconut oil or ghee in a large saucepan that has a tight-fitting lid over medium–high heat. When hot, add the mustard seeds and the chana dhal. When the mustard seeds begin to pop, add the urad dhal and stir well. Add the cinnamon stick, cardamom pods, curry leaves, dried chillies, green chillies and coconut flakes, if using. Fry until the dhal becomes lightly browned in colour, about 2 minutes, then stir in the strained, rinsed rice and coat with the oil.

Top with 750ml (3 cups) water and the coconut milk. Cover the pan and bring to the boil. When it boils, remove from the heat and let it sit undisturbed for 40 minutes.

To serve, carefully separate the rice grains with a fork. Never stir the Basmati rice vigorously as the grains will split. Season with salt to taste.

GHEE RICE

SERVES 2–3

The first time I tried ghee rice, the waiter took a ladleful of melted ghee and drizzled it all over the aromatic rice at the table. This is my somewhat lighter version but it still has a lot of ghee. Treat yourself! You will need a 2-litre (2-quart) saucepan with a tight-fitting lid.

PREP TIME: 20 MINS, PLUS SOAKING TIME
COOKING TIME: 50 MINS

185g (1 cup) Basmati rice
5 tbsp ghee or vegetable ghee, plus a little more to finish
½ onion, finely sliced
1 small piece of mace
2.5cm (1in) piece of cinnamon stick
4 green cardamom pods, lightly smashed
3 cloves
5 curry leaves
1 heaped tbsp garlic and ginger paste
1 tsp salt
10 cashews

Rinse the rice in several changes of cold water until the water runs almost clear. Cover with clean water and allow to soak for 30 minutes.

Melt 3 tablespoons of the ghee over medium–high heat. When hot, fry the onion until lightly browned, about 5 minutes. Transfer the onion to a plate, leaving as much ghee as possible in the pan. Add the mace, cinnamon, cardamom, cloves and curry leaves to the ghee and temper for about 30 seconds. Return half of the onion to the pan.

Strain the soaked rice through a sieve. Stir the garlic and ginger paste, salt and rice into the pan with the spices. Ensure the rice is evenly coated with the ghee and then top with 375ml (1½ cups) cold water. Cover the pan with a tight-fitting lid and bring to the boil. Turn off the heat and leave to steam for 40 minutes. Do not lift the lid!

Meanwhile, fry the cashews in the remaining ghee until golden brown, about 3–5 minutes.

When the rice has steamed, lift the lid and stir carefully with a fork to separate the grains. Never stir Basmati rice roughly as it will split the grains and make it mushy.

To finish, pour the ghee and cashews over the top and stir in the remaining fried onions.

DESSERTS

Indian desserts don't get much attention, but there are some really delicious traditional treats that make a wonderful way to finish off a curry feast. The desserts here are all quite light so you don't need to worry about overindulging.

GF

CHOCOLATE AND CHILLI ICE CREAM

SERVES 4–6
MAKES 1½ LITRES (1.5 QUARTS)

The idea of spicy ice cream might sound a bit odd but, believe me, it's really good! If you don't have an ice cream maker, you can place the mixed ice cream custard in the freezer and give it a good stir every 20 minutes until frozen. That takes longer, though, about six hours – I think I'd be tempted to just buy some good-quality chocolate ice cream and stir in the chilli and whiskey!

PREP TIME: 10 MINS, PLUS 30 MINS CHURNING
COOKING TIME: 15 MINS

- 375ml (1½ cups) double (heavy) cream
- 375ml (1½ cups) whole milk
- 2 tbsp sugar (more or less to taste)
- 3 egg yolks
- 150g (5½oz) best-quality sweetened dark chocolate, broken into small pieces
- 1 tbsp whiskey
- 1–2 tsp chilli powder

Pour the cream, milk and 1 tablespoon of the sugar into a saucepan. Bring to a simmer over medium heat, then reduce the heat slightly.

Meanwhile, whisk the yolks until they become creamy smooth. Add the remaining 1 tablespoon of sugar and then whisk a little more.

Pour the egg yolks into the saucepan. Do not allow it to bubble as the yolks will curdle. Simply cook it over low heat until the mixture is thick enough to coat the back of a spoon, about 6–8 minutes. Don't rush this! It can take some time and if you turn the heat up too much you'll end up with scrambled eggs. If you have a thermometer, the custard should be ready when it reaches 71°C (160°F).

Add the chocolate to the saucepan and stir until it is melted into the cream. Be sure the cream does not get too hot. Add the whiskey and chilli powder and stir to combine. Check for seasoning. I used 2 teaspoons of chilli powder. Allow to cool for a few minutes.

Now pour this into your ice cream maker and turn on the machine. Your ice cream should be ready in about 30 minutes.

CHOCOLATE AND STRAWBERRY 'PANI' PURIS

SERVES 4–6

This is a fun dessert to serve and it really only takes minutes to make. When I prepare a curry feast at home for friends, people are usually quite full by the time it comes to dessert. This one isn't really filling and is a nice way to finish off the meal. For best results, make your own chocolate and chilli ice cream (see page 143). If you're in a rush, use good-quality chocolate ice cream and stir in chilli powder to taste. I first tried these dessert-style pani puris at Zindiya in Birmingham and now I'm hooked! You can use the chocolate bar of your choice. I prefer dark chocolate, but milk chocolate is good, too. Small glasses or even shot glasses will work well for presentation.

PREP TIME: 15 MINS, PLUS CHILLING TIME
COOKING TIME: 10 MINS

- 300g (10½oz) good-quality chocolate
- 20 puri shells (more or less)
- 3 large scoops chocolate and chilli ice cream (see overleaf)
- 15 strawberries
- 1 tbsp icing (powdered) sugar

Roughly chop the chocolate into 1cm (½in) pieces. Place the chopped chocolate in a heatproof bowl. Bring about 3cm (1¼in) of water to a simmer in a saucepan that is slightly smaller than the bowl with the chocolate. Set the chocolate bowl on the mouth of the saucepan, making sure that the water is not touching the bottom of the bowl. Stir the chocolate until it is about 90% melted and take off the heat. The residual heat will melt the rest of the chocolate.

Place a piece of parchment paper on a baking tray. Dip your puris into the melted chocolate so that they are nicely coated, then set them on the parchment paper and place in the freezer to harden for about 30 minutes. If you place the chocolate-coated puris in an air-tight bag, they will keep in the freezer for at least a week.

To finish the dish, melt the ice cream but ensure that it is still very cold. Pour it equally into 4–6 small glasses. This can all be done ahead of time and placed in the coolest part of your fridge. When ready to serve, cut the strawberries into halves or quarters and fill the chocolate coated puris with them. Place the puris on top of the chocolate-filled glasses and sift the icing (powdered) sugar over the top. You can now pour the cold melted ice cream over the strawberries and pop the whole thing into your mouth. Sweet, spicy, chocolatey and crunchy... this one you have to try!

MAKE IT VEGAN

Use a dairy-free chocolate and a vegan ice cream.

APPLE PIE SAMOSAS

MAKES 10

I love a good apple pie, and these miniature samosa pies are always a big hit around my house. They are simple but delicious. They can be made ahead of time and then placed in the oven while you serve dinner.

PREP TIME: 20 MINS
COOKING TIME: 30 MINS

2 tbsp unsalted butter
2 tbsp sugar
3 apples, cored, peeled and diced
1 tsp ground cinnamon
1 tsp cornflour (cornstarch)
1 x 375g (13oz) pack ready-rolled shortcrust pasty
1 egg, beaten
Whipped cream or ice cream, to serve (optional)

TOPPING
1 tbsp ground cinnamon
1 tbsp sugar

Preheat your oven to 200°C (400°F/Gas 6).

Melt the butter in a small pan over medium–high heat. When melted, pour in the sugar and stir until it dissolves in the butter. Tip your apples into the butter mixture. Add the teaspoon of cinnamon and 1 tablespoon of water. Cover the pan and cook until the apple pieces are soft but not mushy, about 15 minutes.

Now mix the cornflour (cornstarch) with the 2 teaspoons of water and stir to combine. Pour this into the apple mixture. Cook for another 1–2 minutes to thicken and cook off the raw flavour of the flour. Once thickened, allow the apple mixture to cool slightly.

Divide the pastry into ten equal-sized pieces. Then roll them out into long thin rectangles. Place a spoonful of the apple mixture in the top left corner of one of the rectangles. Fold this over into a triangle and continue folding until you have a neat triangle shape. Seal by pressing down with your fingers at the seam. It is important that the triangular samosas are tightly sealed so that you don't lose any of the filling when cooking.

Brush the egg wash over each samosa and place in the preheated oven for about 10–15 minutes, until golden brown and hot inside.

For the topping, mix togther the tablespoons of cinnamon and sugar, then sift over the samosas, to taste.

Serve hot as they are, with cream or with ice cream if you wish.

MAKE IT VEGAN

Use a vegan pastry and serve with a dairy-free ice cream.

BANANA DOSAS

SERVES 4–6

This is one of the first Indian desserts I made when I started my blog. My youngest daughter and I would whip these up all the time. It was our bonding time and I loved it. She's now a teenager and isn't so interested in making banana dosas with her old man anymore. But sometimes I still make these and surprise her after dinner. Banana dosas are good on their own but are also nice with kulfi or ice cream.

PREP TIME: 10 MINS
COOKING TIME: 10 MINS

5 bananas
250g (2 cups) brown rice flour
50g (heaped ⅓ cup) plain (all-purpose) flour
1 tbsp sugar (more or less to taste)
A small pinch of salt
Vegetable oil, for greasing
Runny honey, to serve
Pistachio, cardamom and vanilla kulfi (see page 150), to serve (optionall)

Mash the bananas into a thick mushy paste in a large bowl. Kids love doing this! Now sift the flours over the bananas and add the sugar and salt. Mix to combine.

Pour about 150ml (scant ⅔ cup) water into a cup and slowly add it to the mixture while stirring with a wooden spoon. You only want to add enough water so that the mixture is smooth but lumpy from the bananas, and so it kind of plops off the fork when scooped up and dropped back into the bowl. It is quite thick.

Take a little bit of the oil and wipe it onto the surface of a non-stick pan. Place the pan over medium heat. When it is hot, add a scoop of the batter. Let the banana dosa cook in the pan for about 4 minutes on the first side, then flip over and cook for 3 minutes on the opposite side. Be careful not to burn the pancake. Keep warm while you make the rest of the pancakes. Of course, if you have a large pan you should be able to cook a few at a time.

Serve drizzled with runny honey, to taste. I like to serve these with pistachio kulfi.

GF

PISTACHIO, CARDAMOM AND VANILLA KULFI

SERVES 4–8

I once made kulfi the traditional way. It was so good but really time consuming. I sat, reducing four litres of milk for four hours. I had a good book to read so I didn't mind but I don't think I'll be doing that again any time soon. It's much easier to use condensed milk. Personally, I think it is just as good as the kulfi produced by large suppliers using more traditional methods.

PREP TIME: 5 MINS, PLUS FREEZING TIME
COOKING TIME: 20 MINS

- 1 litre (4 cups) whole milk
- 200ml (generous ¾ cup) condensed milk
- ½ tsp ground cardamom
- 4 tbsp finely ground pistachios
- 1 tsp vanilla extract, or the beans from 1 vanilla pod
- 1 tsp rose water
- Sugar, to taste (optional)
- 2 tbsp pistachios, roughly chopped, to serve

Place a heavy-bottomed 3-litre (3-quart) saucepan over medium–high heat. Pour in the milk and bring to the boil. Be careful, as when it does boil it will bubble right over, so reduce the heat quickly and allow to simmer, stirring continuously with a wooden or plastic spatula, for about 10 minutes. The milk will thicken as it simmers. Be sure to continue stirring so that the milk doesn't burn to the bottom of the pan.

Whisk in the condensed milk, cardamom, finely ground pistachios, vanilla, rose water and sugar, if using. Remove from the heat and allow to cool. Divide this mixture into kulfi moulds if you have them. I usually just use an old ice cream container. Place in the freezer, tightly covered, for at least 5 hours. Remove from the freezer about 10 minutes before serving to soften a little, and then remove from the kulfi moulds, if using. I remove the kulfi from my ice cream tub and cut it into slices.

To serve, top with the roughly chopped pistachios.

COLD SPICY GRAPES

SERVES 4 OR MORE AS PART OF A MULTI-COURSE MEAL

This is a popular, colourful and healthy Bangladeshi snack. I like to serve this rather unique snack with pre-dinner drinks or as a light dessert. Spicy grapes may sound a bit strange at first but trust me here! It's the perfect way to start or finish an evening meal. I think of them as a healthy version of pop rocks, the exploding sweets you might have enjoyed as a kid.

PREP TIME: 5 MINS

A 500g (1lb 2oz) bunch of seedless green grapes, cut in half
Juice of 1 lemon
A pinch of flaky sea salt
A pinch of chilli powder (add to your own taste)
3 tbsp finely chopped coriander (cilantro)

Wash and place the grapes in a bowl in the fridge until nicely chilled.

Add the rest of the ingredients and mix well.

Enjoy!

TWO EASY FRUIT SALADS

MAKE AS LITTLE OR AS MUCH AS YOU LIKE

Fruit is a nice way to finish a meal. It's colourful and, of course, very good for you. Here are a couple of colourful combos I like to serve together. They may be simple but sometimes the simple things are the best.

PREP TIME: 10 MINS

MIX 1
Strawberries, quartered
Raspberries
Watermelon, peeled and diced
Blueberries
½ tsp red chilli, very finely chopped

MIX 2
Sweet yellow Indian mangos (available in season at Asian shops), peeled, pitted and diced
Blackberries
Honeydew melon, peeled and diced
1 tsp poppy seeds

DRESSING
Lime juice
Sugar or honey, to taste

Place the different fruit mixes in two separate bowls.

Mix together the lime juice and sugar or honey for the dressing, then pour over the bowls of fruit, to taste. Serve chilled.

LIST OF INGREDIENTS

AJWAIN (CAROM) SEEDS Ajwain seeds, also called carom, are not actually seeds but small fruit. They smell a lot like thyme but their flavour is more of a cross between fennel seed and oregano, only much stronger. The have a pungent, bitter flavour and should be used sparingly as they can easily overpower a dish.

AMCHOOR (DRIED MANGO POWDER) Amchoor powder, made from dried and ground mango, has a strong citric flavour and is really good added to tandoori masalas or any curry that benefits from a citric kick. Often, chefs and spice paste/ masala producers substitute citric acid powder for amchoor, which is significantly stronger in flavour.

ASAFOETIDA In its raw powder form, asafoetida smells terrible. Once fried, its aroma and flavour are much more pleasing, like fried onions. This spice is quite strong so it is used sparingly. In India, it is used as a substitute for garlic and onions in areas where consuming these is forbidden for religious reasons. Asafoetida is also an anti-flatulent and is cooked into dhals and bean dishes to ease digestion. Its most common use in British Indian restaurant cooking is to be tempered in oil to make a tarka for dishes such as tarka dhal. If you are gluten-free, please be careful to check the packaging when you purchase asafoetida as some brands contain wheat flour.

BASMATI RICE
The rice you serve with the recipes in this book has got to be Basmati, and white Basmati is by far the preferred rice. It has a nutty flavour and magnificent aroma that only Basmati can offer. When cooked using my recipes, you will achieve a texture that is nice in the mouth, with just a little resistance when chewing, and not at all sticky. Brown Basmati is simply the same rice that has not had the brown outer husk removed. It is slightly chewier than white and has a nuttier flavour and, as the husk has not been not removed, retains more of its natural minerals and vitamins. Personally, I prefer white, but brown is growing on me. Basmati gets better with age so it is important to look for aged Basmati. It is a little more expensive but worth every penny.

BAY LEAVES (INDIAN, WESTERN) Western and Indian bay leaves are different from each other and not interchangeable, as some cookbooks imply. Indian leaves come from the cassia tree and taste like cassia and cinnamon. Western bay leaves are what you probably already use in your spaghetti Bolognese and meat stews, and taste nothing like cinnamon.

BLACK SALT Black salt is a key ingredient in chaat masala. This volcanic salt has a unique flavour and aroma of sulphur. It isn't to everyone's liking but, believe me, the flavour does grow on you. It can be purchased both online and at most Asian grocers.

CARDAMOM (BLACK AND GREEN) By weight, cardamom is the third most expensive spice in the world, beaten to the top spots only by vanilla and saffron. Green cardamom is most often used in British Indian Restaurant cooking, added to garam masalas and tempered whole in oil. The seeds are what impart the flavour so the pods are often lightly crushed before adding to get that flavour into the dish. Black cardamom are bigger and have a significantly stronger, smoky flavour. If you need to substitute one type for the other, use half as many black pods as green.

CHAAT MASALA This is a unique and flavoursome blend of spices which includes Indian black salt, an Indian volcanic rock salt. The salt contains sulphur, which gives it an interesting flavour and aroma. Chaat masala isn't to everyone's liking but I love the stuff! You can purchase it at Asian shops or make your own. My recipe is on page 8.

CASSIA BARK (see cinnamon)

CHILLIES (FRESH) Fresh chillies range in heat from quite mild to numbingly spicy. I usually use green bird's-eye and bullet chillies for the recipes in this book. That said, I do like to experiment with other chillies as they all have their own unique flavour in addition to their spiciness. Fresh chillies can be used simply split down the middle, finely or roughly chopped, or blended into a chilli paste, as my recipes demonstrate.

CHILLI POWDER The preferred chilli powder at most restaurants is Kashmiri chilli powder. It is quite spicy and has a nice flavour too. Kashmiri chilli powder is available at Asian grocers and also some supermarkets. How spicy your curries are is really a personal thing. I use Kashmiri chilli powder in my cooking but you might like to experiment with milder or hotter chilli powders.

CINNAMON Almost all of the cinnamon sold around the world is actually made from cassia bark. More often than not, the labelling is not deceptive, with cassia often labelled 'cinnamon cassia'. Powdered cassia can be used in both savoury and sweet recipes for a nice, warming kick, and tastes almost identical to real cinnamon powder. Although it tastes great, there is a lot of new medical evidence that has demonstrated that cassia in regular doses can cause liver damage. I don't feel there is much to worry about if you only cook with it from time to time, but if you use whole or ground cinnamon regularly, use Ceylon or 'true cinnamon'. It costs a little more and it's what I use.

If you are looking for 'true cinnamon', it will usually be stated on the label. If in doubt, Ceylon 'true cinnamon' is only grown in Sri Lanka, the Seychelles and Madagascar. Cassia bark comes from China and Indonesia.

CLOVES Many good chefs recommend roasting the whole spices for garam masalas separately as some spices smoke faster than other. This is especially so with cloves, which begin smoking very quickly in a hot pan.

COCONUT Fresh coconut is always best. Break into the shell and grate your own or blend the flesh with a little of the coconut water to make coconut cream, which is delicious stirred into curries. Let's face it... doing all that work isn't something most people want to do. Instead, you can use good-quality coconut cream or milk in these recipes. Dried coconut flakes, frozen shredded or desiccated coconut can also be used as suggested in the recipes.

CORIANDER (CILANTRO) Both the leaves and seeds of the coriander plant are used in Indian cooking. The seeds are tempered whole in some curries and also used ground. Coriander seeds are usually a big player in garam masalas. As ground coriander and cumin are often added to curries in equal measures, I usually roast and grind them together so I have them on hand and can add them faster.

The fresh leaves (cilantro to American readers) are used for their distinctive flavour in sauces, raitas, marinades and pickles. They also make an attractive garnish.

CUMIN White cumin seeds have a strong flavour and aroma that are hugely popular in Indian cooking. Cumin is, in fact, the second most popular spice in the world, second only to black pepper. The seeds can be tempered whole and are also nice added whole to many dishes. Ground cumin plays a big part in Indian cookery and is usually added in equal amounts to ground coriander.

CURRY LEAVES Dried curry leaves are more readily available but fresh are much better if you can get hold of them. When using fresh leaves, wash them before using and freeze any leftover leaves in air-tight containers while they are still wet from washing; this will help keep their fresh green colour.

DHAL I love dhal and cook with many different varieties. For this book, I kept it to four so you wouldn't need to go out and purchase multiple types of lentil. You will need chana dhal, split and washed moong dhal, massoor dhal and white split urad dhal for these recipes. White split urad dhal is the same as the black dhal you use to make dhal makhani but the lentils have been split and washed until white, giving the dhal a completely different flavour.

FENNEL SEEDS Fennel seeds have a nice flavour, similar to black liquorice and star anise. Star anise is slightly stronger but I do use the two spices together and also substitute the whole spices for each other if I've run out of one. Fennel seeds can be tempered whole in oil and also added later to a sauce as a ground spice.

FENUGREEK (METHI) This is the intense aroma that often greets you when you enter an Indian restaurant. You can buy fenugreek (methi) as a powder, whole seeds or as dried leaves (kasoori methi). The powder is made from the ground seeds and is quite strong in flavour, so use it sparingly. The seeds are often used to flavour cooking oil and are also soaked and ground to make different batters, like dosa and idli batter.

The leaves are also used and have a much milder flavour. Fresh fenugreek leaves are often blended and used to flavour sauces and marinades. Dried fenugreek also has a mild flavour and aroma. For best results, dried fenugreek should be added at the end of cooking by rubbing the leaves between your fingers.

FINE SEV Fine sev is used a lot to top and garnish chaats. It is also called nylon sev. It's made from gram (chickpea) flour and looks a lot like tiny pieces of angel hair pasta. You can purchase it at many Asian shops and also online to add a nice crunch to your chaats. If you can't find it, you could use another crispy gram flour-fried noodle or puffed balls of gram flour called bundi, which is easier to find.

GARLIC Garlic is usually best when fresh and freshly prepared. You can use jarred garlic paste and garlic and ginger paste but the flavour is much better if you chop and blend it yourself. When shopping for fresh garlic, look for hard bulbs with tight skin. Although garlic is usually blended into a paste in Indian cookery, it can also be finely chopped or cut into slivers. Don't throw out your old garlic! Older cloves are best for pickles, as fresh garlic has a tendency to turn blue. If it does turn blue, it is still perfectly edible.

GHEE This is clarified butter but it doesn't taste like homemade clarified butter. They must feed the cows something different over there in India. It is available from Asian grocers, and many supermarkets now stock it. Ghee doesn't need to be refrigerated and lasts indefinitely – or so they say. There was a time when curry house curries were sodden in the stuff. Nowadays, healthier alternatives are being used, like rapeseed (canola) oil, but ghee is still hugely popular and a great way of getting a nice buttery flavour into your dishes. If you're looking for a dairy-free alternative, you're in luck! Vegetable ghee tastes like real ghee and works just as well for cooking.

GINGER Ginger is another must-have ingredient for Indian cooking. It is usually prepared as a paste but can also be finely chopped or julienned, as seen in my recipes. When I'm preparing ginger paste, I clean the ginger, then grind it in the skin; the skin has a lot of flavour so shouldn't be wasted. I usually add garlic and ginger in equal measures, though ginger is stronger than garlic. Many chefs add more garlic than ginger for this reason.

GUNPOWDER There are many recipes for gunpowder, which is also called a 'podi'. It's so good it's addictive! My recipe is on page 92.

JAGGERY Jaggery is unrefined sugar that usually comes in large chunks. You can grate or chop it quite easily. You could just use the easier to find light brown sugar.

KURMURE (PUFFED RICE) This looks a lot like Rice Krispies. In fact, I have substituted unsweeted puffed rice cereal for the bhel puri recipe on page 35 and it worked almost as well. It is available at most Asian/Indian grocers.

MUSTARD OIL There's no substitute for mustard oil. It has a pungent and strong flavour and has been used for centuries in northern Indian and Bangladeshi cooking. Although I admit I don't always go to the trouble, it should be heated to smoking point and then cooled before using in cooking or adding to raw ingredients. It isn't good for you but it is used a lot at curry houses as well as high-end restaurants.

MUSTARD SEEDS (BLACK) Mustard seeds are available as black or yellow, but I use the black variety in the recipes in this book, which need to be tempered in very hot oil. Once they start popping, the heat can be reduced and their pungent flavour will be released into the oil. Mustard seeds require this high heat but most whole spices don't. Once the mustard seeds have begun popping in the oil, other whole spices with lower smoking points can be added.

NIGELLA SEEDS (BLACK ONION SEEDS) Although nigella seeds are often called black onion seeds, they aren't actually from the onion family. Whatever you call them, they are excellent sprinkled over homemade naans.

ONIONS One of the first jobs a beginner chef is given when starting out at a curry house is peeling and chopping the onions – lots of them. This is a mundane chore as so many onions are required – they're used in almost everything. Although I do use shallots and red onions in some recipes, the onions you will need for most dishes are the medium- to large-sized Spanish onions found everywhere. I recommend purchasing large bags from Asian grocers, which is much less expensive than purchasing in smaller quantities.

PANEER This is the most simple of cheeses. It is neutral in flavour, like cottage cheese, and comes in blocks. Indian paneer is now widely available in Asian shops and in supermarkets. For the recipes in this book, commercially bought paneer will do fine, but you can also make your own (see page 26).

PAPRIKA Paprika, both sweet and hot, is used in a lot of curries. It is popular for its pungent flavour and deep red colour. It can be used in place of chilli powder if you want a nice red colour without all the heat.

RAPESEED (CANOLA) OIL This is my oil of choice for Indian meals. I find some other vegetable oils, like those produced with soy, have a strong flavour that simply isn't as good. Rapeseed oil is also healthier than other vegetable oils and is ideal for cooking over a high heat as it has a high smoking point, making it perfect for deep- and shallow-frying. Rapeseed oil is often labelled 'vegetable oil', so be sure to check the packaging – look for vegetable oil made from rapeseed. Avoid fancy cold-pressed rapeseed oil, as it is expensive and doesn't have a high smoking point.

ROSE WATER Rose water is made by steeping rose petals in water. It's cheap so there's no need to go picking rose petals. This fragrant water is added to rice, biryanis, kormas and other dishes to make them taste and smell even better.

SAFFRON By weight, saffron is the most expensive spice on the planet, worth more than gold. Luckily, you don't need a lot, as a little goes a long way. Saffron consists of the stigma of the crocus flower. Only three stigma grow on each flower, which have to be picked by hand. That's why it's so expensive. Many restaurants use turmeric instead of saffron to give their food colour. I use saffron threads, which add a much better flavour than powdered saffron.

SALT Although fine table salt is used in most restaurants, I prefer to use flaky salt, such as Maldon, when seasoning a dish before serving. It just looks better. In my recipes, I rarely give an exact measure of salt as I feel this is a personal choice. One thing I would like to stress is that the spices in curries need a good dose of salt to bring out their flavour.

STAR ANISE This spice is popular all over Asia. It has a distinctive liquorice flavour, stronger than fennel seeds. I use fennel and star anise in many of my spice masalas.

TAMARIND Tamarind is available both in block form and as a concentrated paste. I used to just use shop-bought tamarind concentrate for ease but have found the flavour to be much better when I make my own using block tamarind. I give instructions on how to do this on page 10; just follow the first two paragraphs.

TINDAS Also known as an Indian squash or round gourd, this is a strange vegetable that tastes really good. You'll probably have to go to an Asian shop to find tindas, but they are worth the trip. They are often called baby pumpkins, but they aren't pumpkins at all. That said, you could substitute pumpkin for the tindas in my tinda curry recipe on page 51. It will be different in flavour and texture but still very good.

TOMATOES (FRESH, CANNED, PASTE, PURÉE) Tomatoes are used in a number of ways in British Indian restaurant and authentic subcontinent curries, sauces and raitas. Fresh tomatoes are good diced or quartered to add flavour, colour and texture. When chopped tomatoes are required, I use fresh when they are in season and tinned (canned) when not. Tinned are really good and I use them a lot. If you prefer a smoother curry house-style sauce, try using blended tomatoes or passatta instead of chopped, or use a combination of the two.

TURMERIC Turmeric is one of the spices that make Indian food what it is. It has a distinctive woody, bitter flavour that is popular in curries and rice. It is often used as a substitute for saffron, for its colour, though it tastes nothing like it. Its deep yellow colour gives food an appetizing appearance, but as it is quite bitter, it is used sparingly.

YOGHURT (GREEK, PLAIN) You may have read Indian cookbooks calling for well-hung yoghurt. This yoghurt is wrapped in muslin (cheesecloth) to drain excess whey, making it thicker. I use full-fat Greek yoghurt for marinating paneer and vegetables, just as it is used in most Indian restaurants. I also prepare thick raitas with it. For thinner raitas and for use in sauces, I use plain natural yoghurt, which doesn't curdle as easily. If you are vegan, there are exceptionally good dairy-free yoghurts made from soy or coconut that are now conveniently available at most supermarkets.

SUPPLIERS

VEGETABLE AND HERB SOURCES

FARMER'S CHOICE

I have used Farmer's Choice since starting writing my blog and it has been a valuable sponsor ever since. It supplies an excellent range of organic fruit and vegetables, as well as a good selection of store-cupboard ingredients, like salt and vegetable stock. This can all be delivered right to your doorstep. I can highly recommend its service.
www.farmerschoice.co.uk

RED DEER HERBS

Red Deer Herbs supplies an impressive range of micro herbs and fresh herbs and chillies. If you're looking for fresh curry leaves, they even supply those!
https://reddeerherbs.co.uk/

PLANTS4PRESENTS

Fancy growing your own curry leaves? I've done it, and this is where I got my plants from.
https://plants4presents.co.uk

SPICES, PULSES, RICE AND FLOUR

EAST END FOODS

East End Foods has been a sponsor of my blog for a few years. I have visited its production facilities and know I can trust it to deliver excellent quality spices and Basmati rice. I purchase its whole spices to roast and grind them into my own masala blends but it also supplies good-quality garam masala, curry powder and other pre-ground spices that can come in very handy when you don't want to go to the work of roasting and grinding your own. East End Foods' products are available at many supermarkets, Amazon, Ocado and Asian grocers. It also has a brilliant online shop.
http://store.eastendfoods.co.uk

COOKWARE

SPICES OF INDIA

You will love shopping on this site. In addition to all the groceries and spices it supplies, you will also find a fantastic range of Indian kitchen and tableware.
www.spicesofindia.co.uk

THE BIRMINGHAM BALTI BOWL CO.

Authentic Balti Bowls are once again being manufactured in the UK. The quality is fantastic and you can purchase yours here.
thebirminghambaltibowlco.com

BARBECUE AND GRILLING

THÜROS BARBECUES

If you love kebabs, you've got to check out Thüros Kebab Grills. I love mine.
www.thueros.com

TRAEGER BARBECUES

The easy way to get delicious smoky flavour into your barbecued foods. Traeger barbecues use wood pellets to cook the food. You can set the preferred temperature and let the Traeger do all the work. This is the perfect barbecue for easy indirect cooking.
http://thealfrescochef.co.uk

US SOURCES

PENZEYS

A large range of spices that can be bought online.
www.penzeys.com

SAVORY SPICE

A large range of spices.
www.savoryspiceshop.com

ISHOPINDIAN.COM

Groceries and Indian cooking utensils .
www.ishopindian.com

INDEX

ACKNOWLEDGEMENTS

I have really enjoyed working with everyone at Quadrille over the past few years. As with my first two cookbooks, this book was a real group effort. Thank you to Sarah Lavelle for commissioning this book. Thank you to Louise Francis and Becci Woods for all your input and work along the way. Thanks also go to Nicola Ellis and team for making the book look so nice!

Once again it was my privilege to work with the hugely talented photographer Kris Kirkham. Thanks, Kris! Thank you also to Amber De Florio. You made everything look so good on the page. Thank you to everyone at Quadrille who worked behind the scenes. You understood what I was trying to accomplish with this book and your efforts are very much appreciated.

I am grateful to my wife, Caroline, and kids, Katy, Joe and Jennifer, for trying all my recipes and helping me decide which should go into the book.

This book would have been a lot more difficult to write were it not for the many excellent chefs who have taught me and given me useful tips over the years. I would like to name two restaurants that have most inspired me in the writing of this book. Thank you to the manager of Ury in Newcastle, Ansar Pullani, and head chef Mohammed Mukkath for taking the time to demonstrate recipes and offering advice on making the perfect Indian meal. I love Ury and go there every time I'm in Newcastle. Their food is top notch! I would also like to thank Ajay Kenth, co-owner of Zindiya Streatery and Bar in Birmingham, for pretty much letting me watch them cook every dish they offer on their fantastic menu. What a place! I can't wait to go back.

Lastly, I would like to thank you for picking up this book. I have been so lucky to have met so many great people over the years, through social media and in person, who have purchased my books and offered support and great convo! I hope you enjoy this new collection of recipes. I'm always contactable if you would like to ask any recipe questions or just want to talk food.

Publishing Director: Sarah Lavelle
Project Editor: Louise Francis
Senior Designer: Nicola Ellis
Designer: Monika Adamczyk
Cover Design: Smith & Gilmour
Photographer: Kris Kirkham
Food Stylist: Amber De Florio
Props Stylist: Faye Wears
Production Director: Vincent Smith
Production Controller: Tom Moore

First published in 2019 by Quadrille,
an imprint of Hardie Grant Publishing

Quadrille
52–54 Southwark Street,
London SE1 1UN
quadrille.com

Cataloguing-in-Publication Data. A catalogue record for this book is available from the British Library.

ISBN 978-1-78713-258-0

Printed in China

In five short years Dan took The Curry Guy from an idea to a reliable brand. The recipes are all developed and tested in Dan's home kitchen. And they work. His bestselling first cookbook – *The Curry Guy* – and the 130,000 curry fans who visit his blog every month can testify to that fact.

www.greatcurryrecipes.net | @thecurryguy